RYA Mu  k
s

by Andrew Simpson

Illustrations by the Author

© Andrew Simpson 2010
First Published 2010
The Royal Yachting Association
RYA House, Ensign Way, Hamble
Southampton SO31 4YA
Tel: 0844 556 9555
Fax: 0844 556 9516
E-mail: publications@rya.org.uk
Web: www.rya.org.uk
ISBN: 978-1-906435-42-4
RYA Order Code: G92

Totally Chlorine   Sustainable
Free   Forests

A CIP record of this book is available from the British Library.

Note: While all reasonable care had been taken in the
preparation of this book, the publisher takes no responsibility for
the use of the methods or products or contracts described in the
book.

Cover Design: Design House
Typesetting and Design: Kevin Slater
Proofreading and indexing: Alan Thatcher
Printed in China through World Print
Photo credits: Cover David Harding

FOREWORD

Multihulls have come a long way since the sailors of the Indian and South Pacific Oceans came up with the cunning concept of lashing two canoes together in order to form a more stable platform on which to sail. If there is one common thread throughout the history of multihull sailing, however, it is that it has always been a lot of fun.

It is also fair to say that they have a fairly unique set of handling characteristics which you need to get your head around before you can fully enjoy these boats and the RYA Multihull Handbook is an excellent starting point for anyone wanting to get involved in this exhilarating form of the sport of sailing.

I myself have long been a convert to the benefits of two hulls as opposed to one, having owned a cruising cat for many years. I would have to say that I found Andrew Simpson's clear and concise guide a very useful and illuminating handbook.

Whether it's getting to grips with the very basics of multihull stability, right through to the fundamentals of handling a multihull under power or sail, this book has it covered. It is also really nice to read a book which tackles some of the skills that many of us cat sailors have had to learn through the old methods of trial and error and scratches and scrapes – I'm talking close quarters boat handling here.

On a more serious note, the pointers on handling a multihull in heavy weather and coping with capsize and man overboard are absolutely invaluable and mean that this authoritative text is an absolute must for any multihull sailor who is serious about heading offshore.

Enjoy this book and, in the meantime, I wish you fair winds and fast passages.

Rod Carr O.B.E.

INTRODUCTION

Let's fantasise. An inventor has come up with a new product he is anxious to sell to the world. He assembles a marketing team to help him promote the idea.

'This is it,' he announces flashing up the first image on the screen.

'What is it?' someone asks.

'It's a boat.'

Patent disbelief from all. 'Really? But it's only got one hull.'

'Ahah! Well spotted. That's why I've called it – wait for it – a monohull. That's 'mono' meaning single, and 'hull' – but, hey, you're probably ahead of me there. Anyway, it's your job to advise me how we can exploit its many advantages.'

'What advantages?'

'Well, for starters, it would take up less space in marinas.'

'But, with only one hull, won't it fall over?'

'Now, here's the clever bit,' cried the inventor, his eyes gleaming. 'What I've done is place a lump of lead low beneath the hull on a sort of fin thing. That holds it upright.'

'So marinas would need to be deeper?'

'Yes, but only a little. Three or four metres should do it.'

The head marketing man was thoughtfully tapping his teeth with a pencil. 'I see. But going back to the lead. Presumably that would make your monohull both heavier and slower...'

'Absolutely.'

'... in which case we could plug the point that passage times would be longer, giving you more time to relish the experience.'

The inventor was jubilant. 'Excellent. I knew you were the guys for the job.'

'But we'll need more,' opined another. 'Something more thrilling. Any ideas?'

The inventor looked thoughtful. 'There is one thing. My prototype tends to lean over when sailing. I call it 'heeling'. It's really lots of fun, particularly when the cups and saucers start flying about.'

'Which brings me to the safety aspect…'

Somebody yawned. 'The crockery has fantastic potential, but safety doesn't sell. Not sexy enough. Do tell us about it anyway.'

'Well, you see my monohull can't be capsized. If it rolls over it just bobs right back upright again. Surely we can make something of that?

'Hmm. Pretty feeble. Where's the fun in not capsizing? But hang on a second – what about sinking? If it were holed would it go to the bottom?'

'You bet. Like a stone.'

'Then – wow! – I think we're onto a winner here. Can only float in deep water, sails slower than a glacier going uphill, the excitement of crashing crocks – toss in a few carving knives, some heavy books and a sprinkling of battery acid there – and then, as a clincher, if your boat sinks you might even have to swim the last miles of your voyage.'

You might have guessed that this is just a fable but it serves to illustrate how standpoint can challenge accepted wisdom and practice. One person's logic can be another's folly and it's possible for opposing sides in an intellectual conflict never to fully understand the other's point of view. This was a problem when western designers first started to develop 'modern' variations on the multihull theme during the late 1950s and into the '60s and '70s. There was considerable scepticism, some animosity, and a great deal of hot air wasted on explaining how intrinsically unsafe – irresponsible even – were these bizarre new creations.

Thankfully, for multihulls there's nothing more to prove. They have become respectable. Yes, they have their own particular characteristics and vulnerabilities, but they are not alone there since this is true of all boats. It's all a matter of understanding how they work and how to get the best of them.

Which is what this book is all about.

Andrew Simpson

CONTENTS

CHAPTER 1

HOW IT ALL BEGAN

The word catamaran comes from the Tamil kattu-maram meaning tied wood, a fact that gives a strong clue to the geographical origins of this ancient type of craft. The Tamil language is spoken mainly in southern India and north-eastern Sri Lanka, where simple craft having a central hull and either a single or a pair of stabilising outriggers are used to this day. But this isn't the only region where multi-hulled vessels have a long history. Over the centuries they have been used extensively through Indonesia and over much of the Pacific – Polynesia, Micronesia and Melanesia – spreading outwards from the East Asian coast and sequentially colonising the islands that dot this vast oceanic space, as far east as Easter Island southwards to New Zealand, there to establish the Maori culture. Not all of these boats were small. Large double-hulled canoes capable of carrying several families at a time became a popular mode of transport. No one knows the time span involved, but it's somewhere in the order of tens of thousands of years.

Construction of these rickety craft was relatively crude with the technology developing only very slowly. In smaller examples, the main hull was often a dugout and the outriggers solid logs, roughly shaped, all joined together by spindly beams, often of bamboo. In the absence of any other type of fastening, the structures were bound together with lashings braided or twisted from natural fibres – coconut husks and hibiscus bark being popular sources. There was little attempt to keep the water out of the hulls. In such warm seas, why bother?

These early vessels may seem primitive from our modern point of view but they certainly weren't impractical. Being inherently flexible they absorbed rather than resisted the stresses induced by wave action, thereby adopting a structurally sympathetic principle well understood by engineers today. And, of course, when your spares kit comprised a few extra sticks and a hank of twine, running repairs were a matter of little consequence, even on passage.

Built in 1876, Herreshoff's catamaran *Amaryllis* still looks surprisingly modern today

It would be easy to imagine that modern multihulls emerged via the antics of wild-eyed eccentrics, rather like the early days of aviation when all sorts of daft ideas were explored. This was not the case. In 1876 the illustrious American naval architect, Nathanael Herreshoff – designer of no less than five America's Cup winners – designed (and patented) the 10m (33ft) catamaran, *Amaryllis*. At a Centennial Regatta at the New York Yacht Club

RYA Multihull Handbook for cruisers

This James Wharram designed catamaran is a true descendent of ancient traditions

she took on all-comers, including many much larger yachts, and comprehensively humiliated them. A contemporary report tells us that '… she fairly flew along the Long Island shore, passing yacht after yacht as if they were anchored.' Unsurprisingly, this didn't sit well with the club worthies and, although she was grudgingly awarded line honours on that occasion, *Amaryllis* soon found herself banned from competing. Herreshoff did build at least one more catamaran but, no doubt sensing which way the commercial wind blew, soon abandoned his experiments and returned to his more conventional practice.

1947 saw pioneer surfer Woodbridge (Woody) Brown build the 11.6m (38ft) and scarily narrow-beamed catamaran *Manukai* (Sea Bird) in Hawaii. His assistant was a Hawaiian – Rudy Choy – who, after moving to California, went on to design some spectacularly successful cats of his own.

At roughly the same time in England, brothers Roland and Francis Prout – both Olympic kayakers – were experimenting with a couple of canoes lashed together. After competing in the 1952 Helsinki Olympics, they returned to the theme with more serious intent. 1954 saw the arrival of the 5.05m (16ft 6in) *Shearwater*, an inspired twin-hulled dinghy that was to open the door for so many small racing cats that followed. The brothers later turned their attention to larger cruising catamarans, of which we shall hear much more later in this book, and their name still resonates through the multihull world.

By the 1960s the fuse was well and truly lit under an exploding interest in multihulls. In California ex-pilot Arthur Piver was marketing plans for his somewhat boxy trimarans. In Australia Hedley Nicol was doing much the same thing. And others at that time were also making a name for themselves, amongst them: Dick Newick, Jim Brown and Norman Cross in the US; Derek Kelsall, Bill O'Brien and James Wharram in Britain, and Lock Crowther in Australia. Even I had a hand in those barnstorming days, launching my first trimaran design in 1968 and sailing a slightly larger version in the Round Britain Race of 1970.

One thing was certain: there was no turning back. Multihulls were here to stay.

2

MULTIHULLS:
GETTING TO KNOW THEM

Catamaran enthusiasts will have you believe that there are only three types of boat: catamarans, half catamarans and catamarans-and-a-half – meaning cats, monohulls and trimarans respectively. However, the rest of the world sees things from a rather less skewed perspective so perhaps it would be safer if we went along with the majority view.

Catamarans

These are twin-hulled craft which, like all multihulls, depend mainly on their beam for stability. I use the word 'mainly' because smaller racing cats use crew weight as ballast, in many instances employing trapeze wires to get that human ballast where it will do the most good – as far outboard as possible. The whole issue of stability will be discussed in Chapter 3 but, since this is a book about multis with seagoing potential, for now let's simply accept that, for larger boats, it's their wide stance that keeps them upright.

Lots of deck space...

... and spacious interiors. No wonder catamarans are so popular

Catamarans are by far the most popular form of cruising multihull. Compared with trimarans – at least the non-folding type – they are less beamy and generally provide more accommodation, length for length, than their three-hulled cousins. Catamarans are also structurally simpler and, therefore, easier and cheaper to build – a winning argument when it comes to commercial production.

The combination of lots of habitable space wrapped in a relatively uncomplicated envelope has in many instances been overexploited, giving rise to what are sometimes derisively known as roomarans – those in which accommodation has been gained at the cost of sailing performance.

This might be a good time to explode a popular myth which we will expand on in the next chapter. The notion that multihulls are automatically faster than monohulls simply isn't true. Keelboat design has advanced immensely over the past couple of decades, making even cruising examples much slipperier than they once were. Yet, although the performance gap may have narrowed, the potential for enjoying a superior speed advantage still rests with multihulls. But this can easily be lost by having too much weight and windage. Of course, to choose a boat because it offers the accommodation of a small hotel and stowage to match is a perfectly legitimate aim in its own right. Just don't expect breathtaking speed as part of the package.

Larger catamarans are usually integrated structures but the smaller ones are often made up of individual hulls joined by crossbeams, with trampolines or slatted decks slung between them. The latter type can usually be demounted for transportation overland.

Trimarans

It is said that the word trimaran was coined by Victor Tchetchet, once a fighter pilot for the last Russian Czar and later an ardent US-based multihull enthusiast. It describes an unballasted boat having a centre hull, stabilised on either side by smaller hulls – a concept recognisable to the Polynesians over several thousands of years.

With its 'wings' folded, this Ian Farrier designed trimaran can occupy a normal-sized marina berth

Not only has the concept survived but so have fragments of the language – at least in some quarters. For example, there are those who like to refer to the outer hulls as amas and the beams that tie them together as akas. With apologies to the purists, I must acknowledge that I'm not amongst them. I find the words too confusing. Not only are they very much alike but ama also means the port hull of a double canoe – i.e., a catamaran. So, in the interests of unambiguity, from now on in this book I'll be sticking with plain English. The outer hulls will be called floats or outriggers and the connecting structures beams. Hulls will remain … well, hulls.

As with catamarans, trimarans ('tris' for short) can either be unified, seamless structures – though may still have open wind decks – or be demountable for transport and storage ashore. Some designs employ mechanisms, varying in ingenuity, that allow the floats to be folded alongside the hull to reduce the beam. Unfortunately, this clearly worthwhile feature can only be applied to smaller boats, since the weight of the floats and the loads on the beams increase dramatically with size. The engineering simply becomes impracticable and unaffordable.

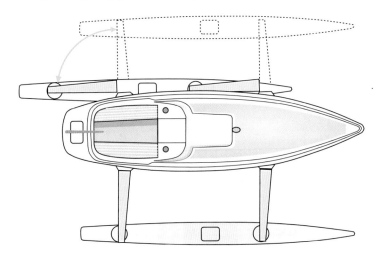

Some designs allow the floats to be swung in alongside the centre hull. The beam is reduced but the boat's length increases

Accommodation compared

Small to mid-size tris have their living areas limited to the centre hull, though often extending outboard over the side decks in the form of wing berths. This means they are not as spacious as most catamarans – (or indeed monohulls) of comparable length. Very large trimarans take advantage of all three hulls, making them positively cavernous inside. But, some would say sadly, the species *Trinormous humungous* has pretty well died out, driven into extinction by the big cats.

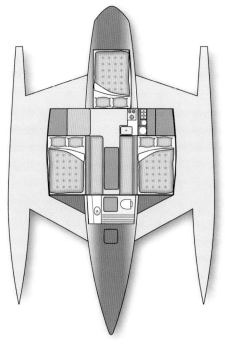

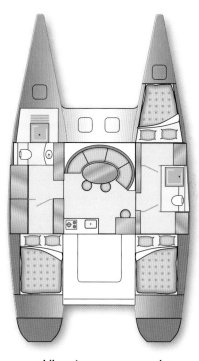

A trimaran's accommodation is concentrated mainly in centre hull...

... while catamarans can make use of the entire beam

Being sited on the centreline and more or less at water level, a trimaran's accommodation in some ways resembles a monohull's. This location places the crew very near to the roll centre – the axis around which a boat heels. Granted, multihulls aren't much into heeling, but some is unavoidable. And for the crew, the further you are from the roll centre, either vertically or laterally, the greater will be the effects of roll, however modest. Sometimes these effects can be bizarre.

On a cross-Channel passage, skippering a catamaran I had never sailed before. We were on passage from Falmouth to the Chenal du Four, I was off-watch and in my bunk at the after end of the starboard hull. The conditions were brisk but not threatening. As the boat rose to each wave, I felt myself being jerked upwards. But there was never any corresponding sensation of descending again. This was hugely disconcerting. Convinced that the hull was being progressively jacked into the air in small increments, I had to take myself on deck to reassure myself that we weren't capsizing.

How do they handle?

My own opinion is that tris are rather more fun to sail than cats. With only a single rudder (usually) and simpler, more direct steering linkages, the person at the helm enjoys the kind of 'feel' normally found in dinghies – with none of that griping and rounding-up dinghies get with extreme angle of heel. By contrast, catamarans with their twin rudders, sometimes with dual steering positions, are often obliged to have complex steering systems that are unresponsive by comparison.

Another area where trimarans score is that they sit lower in the water than most cats and, as a consequence, have less windage. This, and the relatively shallow draught of their floats means they tack more readily, pirouetting around their centre hulls with aplomb.

If you want to combine cruising with some sailing thrills, nothing beats a trimaran for responsiveness and excitement

But these, of course, are generalisations. There are cantankerous tris and wonderfully house-trained cats. A great deal has to do with the quality of the design.

It might be tempting to conclude that I favour trimarans, but this would be to overstate the case. The fact that cats so vastly outnumber tris is no accident, since they bring so many practical advantages to the feast, generally offering more for the money and being less expensive to build. This being the case it's unsurprising that so few manufacturers have adopted the triple-hulled option – the exceptions being a handful of independently minded companies who either custom build flat out ocean racers or manufacture folding and demountable designs to serve a limited but loyal niche market. Nonetheless, for those who sail shorthanded and have no call for roomy accommodation in the compartmentalised layouts so typical of cats, the trimaran still has much to offer.

CHAPTER 3

SOME MULTIHULL MATHS

In discussions about multihulls the two topics that tend to dominate are speed (a laudable attribute) and capsize (ah, well, there had to be a catch somewhere). In many instances the rewards of the former and the menace of the latter are exaggerated, with little appreciation of the underlying factors.
To gain a more insightful perspective we must delve a little deeper.

All are not equal

Before we get too immersed in details it's important to understand that physical properties don't always vary directly with boat size, thanks to what's known as 'the law of mechanical similitude' – a conversation stopper of a phrase that describes a scaling law that's central to our understanding of how boats work and what we can expect from them. The principle is best explained by example.
Let's take a boat of any length and scale it up to exactly twice its original size. It would be tempting to think that its various dimensional properties would simply double and, indeed, some do. But not all.

- Linear measurements such as length, beam and draught vary in proportion to the scaling factor. The results of doubling the size being: twice the length, twice the beam and twice the draught.
- Those values that involve areas, such as wetted surface and sail areas, vary as the square.
- Anything that has a volume, like displacement, varies with the cube. So, incidentally, does the heeling effect of wind velocity on the sails.
- Stability varies by the power of four.

So, what does this mean numerically?

If we double the size of a boat we get:
- Twice the length, beam and draught (x 2)
- Four times wetted surface and sail areas. (2 x 2 = 4)
- Eight times the displacement and heeling effect. (2 x 2 x 2 = 8)
- Sixteen times the stability (2 x 2 x 2 x 2 = 16)

Of course, it would be absurd to scale up a design in such a simplistic manner. After all, we can expect people who sail small boats to be roughly the same height as those who sail larger ones, so there's no need to have twice the headroom. But these dimensional relationships give us an important, though inexact, means of comparing the properties of boats of different sizes. If say, comparing a 10m (33ft) cat with one of 20m (66ft) we might deduce that the larger boat would have roughly four times the accommodation area and be sixteen times more stable – two very significant advantages that go with size. And, since build costs roughly follow displacement, we could guess that the larger vessel is also likely to be eight times more expensive!

Incidentally, it was the law of mechanical similitude that helped kill off commercial sailing ships. Faced with a growing threat from steam, they struggled to compete by building bigger and bigger ships – only to hit the mechanical similitude wall head on. With displacement advancing by the cube and sail area only by the square, they soon found they couldn't set enough sail to propel all that added weight. Bizarre five- and six-masted schooners were their last desperate attempts. Meanwhile, steamers were discovering that they could carry more cargo (cube) for relatively less wetted surface area (square) so, for them, big was definitely beautiful. Game, set and match to mechanisation and a sad end to a glorious maritime era.

Stability

This is one of those subjects that's very simple in theory, becoming almost impossible to pin down when placed in context – at sea, with all the variables that heaving environment implies. When figures are quoted, they usually refer to static stability which assumes a stationary boat parked on a motionless sea.

'Not very realistic,' I hear you mutter, and you would be right. But at least it gives us a means to compare one multihull with another and to distinguish between those that are very stable and those that exist on the ragged edge.

Stability involves a battle between moments – not moments of passion or sadness or other transient sensations, but moments of force where a force acts on a lever arm to produce torque, as we might use a spanner (left).

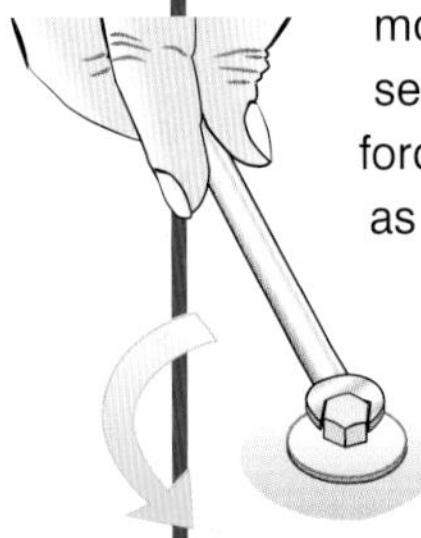

In the stability battle the two protagonists are the heeling moment and the righting moment which are derived thus:

fig 3:1

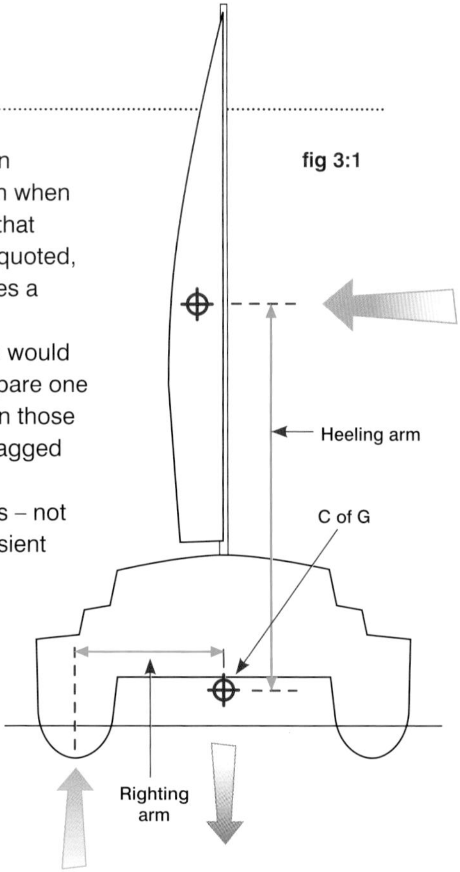

Heeling arm

C of G

Righting arm

Heeling moment: The force here is that of the wind, which can be thought of as acting through what's known as the Centre of Effort (for practical purposes the geometric centre of the sailplan). The lever is the height of CE above the boat's Centre of Gravity (CG).

Righting moment: Here the force is the weight of the boat acting downwards through CG. The lever is basically half the beam – more specifically the horizontal distance between CG and the centreline of a catamaran's hull or a trimaran's float. Note that overall beam is never used. This is because some hulls flare outwards above the waterline, and this would distort the calculations.

RYA Multihull Handbook for cruisers

STABILITY FACTOR

One of the most useful measures of stability estimates a Stability Factor, meaning the apparent windspeed in knots at which a catamaran starts lifting a hull – in other words, the point when the need to reduce sail becomes urgent. The formula works for cats and most tris:

$$SF = 8.24 \sqrt{\frac{0.5 \times B \times d}{SA \times CE}}$$

Where:
SF = windspeed in knots when a multihull must reef
B = beam between the centrelines of outer hulls (feet)
d = displacement (lbs)
SA = Sail area (square feet)
CE = height of Centre of Effort above CG (feet)

3

Expressed at its simplest, multihull stability depends on beam and weight. The heavier a boat and the wider it is, the more stable it will be.

Submersible float trimarans

This concept was popular around the 1970s but has since fallen out of fashion. The phrase submersible float is self-explanatory. It describes a float having insufficient buoyancy to bear the total weight of the boat – about 90% was my preference, since I was one its advocates. The reasoning was undeniably logical – though had its flaws as we'll find out soon. If overpressed by a gust, went the theory, the float submerges and the boat heels, thereby spilling the wind from the sails – rather like a monohull knocked down in a squall. Trimarans in general and this type in particular tend to have a less snappy motion than catamarans. I know sailors who have been converted from one to another for just this reason.

With submersible float tris, the force component in our righting moment is no longer the weight of the boat, but becomes the displacement of the float – that's to say the upward thrust of its buoyancy (fig 3:2). In these circumstances, the SF formula must be adapted by substituting float buoyancy for displacement.

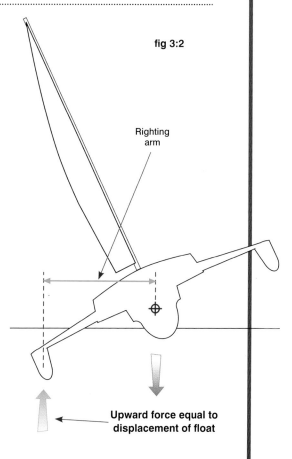

fig 3:2

Righting arm

Upward force equal to displacement of float

Stability in motion

The weakness in all discussions on stability lies in the fact that much of what we assume – even hold to be essential truths – is pure conjecture. Guesswork, in other words. Working out the stability factor might give us a nice warm feeling but, at the end of the day, we face a watery world containing so many variables that almost anything can happen.

Let's go back to our submersible float trimarans. As we've just read, the motives behind the thinking were to make this type more resistant to capsize by having them bury a float rather than rotate around it.

One problem was that nobody contacted the sea gods to tell them of the plan. To confound our theories, boats of this type actually did capsize – whether more or less readily than high volume float designs isn't on record but, equally, there was no clear evidence of extra protection.

It's difficult to know quite why this was so but, at the risk of straying even deeper into guesswork, it's probable that: a) the float didn't submerge quickly enough to save the boat or: b) the float was at least partially planing at the time – i.e. supported by dynamic lift in the manner of a water skier and therefore effectively behaving like a high buoyancy float.

One learned analysis on stability concludes that it's impossible for a catamaran to be flipped by wave action alone. Now, I have no problems with the general thrust of the reasoning employed but 'impossible' seems a rather bold assertion. Isn't that what they said about the *Titanic* vis-à-vis sinking?

If there is one sure truth it is that there are precious few absolute truths, and we should be wary of any claims that there are. The dynamics of stability (and its mercifully infrequent failure – capsize) are extremely complicated and only in part quantifiable. We have to accept that a boat in motion is going to behave differently than one at rest. We simply don't always know what will be thrown at us, nor how we should handle it. This is both the challenge and risk we take when going sailing.

We shall be dealing with multihull seamanship, including heavy weather sailing and capsize, in Chapters 8 and 9 but let me say in advance that I believe it's the skipper not the designer who has the greatest influence on safety.

'Caution! Stability at rest has little connection with stability in motion. Your boat might be as stiff as a church alongside but could be in serious danger of capsize at speed in rough conditions'

■ **RYA Stability and Buoyancy** (order code G23), offers useful further reading on this subject. www.rya.org.uk/shop

Fast or furious – the quicks and the slows of it

Under the pulse-stirring slogan '30 knots possible', a range of trimarans sprang onto the sailing scene way back in the 1960s. Having sailed both on board and in company with examples of that breed I was rash enough to remark, I'm afraid all too publicly: 'only if dropped by a crane'. I still regret the offence I caused – but not the sentiment. Very few sailboats achieve 30 knots and, sadly, these particular examples stood no risk whatsoever of being candidates.

Plywood was the preferred construction medium back then, and a very fine material it remains. But it came in large sheets and preferred to be used that way, demonstrating a natural reluctance to take up compound curves. Actually, the whole era was known for its boxy boats, mainly swarms of bilge-keeled monos, all built quickly, cheaply and relatively crudely for a nation still emerging from post-war austerity and hungering to get afloat. Hydrodynamics was not the first thing on their mind. And it showed, for some were heartbreakingly inefficient.

The two primary enemies of multihull performance are weight and wetted surface. Let's discuss the last first.

Skin drag

This arises from the friction between the hull surface and the water and is the major drag component at low speeds. The shape that contains the maximum volume for the least wetted surface area is a sphere, but this isn't a practical suggestion for us sailors since there are other criteria to satisfy – namely, that our hulls must also be long and slim, allowing them to slice through the water without fuss.

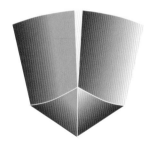

fig 3:3   Wetted surface area decreases the nearer the cross-sectional shape resembles a semicircle. Early multihulls had simple single-chined hulls (red), then evolved via multi-chined (blue) to the typical round bottomed shape (yellow) we know today

However, the sphere does give us a clue as to how to strike the best compromise. Fig 3:3 shows how hull sections evolved since the early days. The first offerings were single chined, with subsequent developments adding a second chine, each step bringing the section ever closer to the ideal, a round-bottomed 'U' – as near to an extruded sphere as you can get while satisfying other conditions. Not only did wetted surface area and skin drag reduce with each refinement but, as a bonus, the water was given a kinder shape to flow around.

Compared to today's fin-keeled monohulls, multihulls tend to be extravagant on wetted surface area. As a hull of any given displacement gets longer and thinner, its surface area – and therefore the skin drag – increases. Consequently, most cruising multihulls should expect to be outsailed by fin-keelers in windspeeds of less than 8 knots or so. In such conditions slender hulls and lightness bring no advantage.

Trimarans with all three hulls immersed will suffer the most, though those capable of flying the windward float can often use crew weight to reduce wetted surface area (fig 3:4). Catamarans are stuck with what they have, though retracting any daggerboards is obviously helpful in these circumstances.

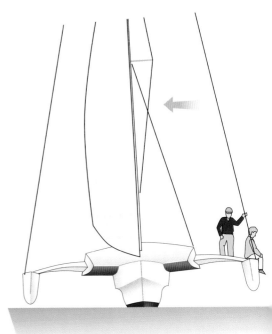

fig 3:4 Some trimarans can be balanced by crew weight so only the centre hull remains immersed

Weight

Multihull skippers face almost unbearable temptation. Confronted by a veritable surfeit of internal volume, it seems to go against nature to leave it empty. A couple of folding bicycles? No problem. An inflatable kayak? In the port bow. How about a few deckchairs for party time? Now, that's great idea! And so on.

It has to be said that multihullers are not alone in succumbing to squirreling instincts. All boats – my own included – collect clobber as pockets attract lint. It's just that multihulls present the greatest opportunity, and will experience the most pain if it's overindulged.

And don't think that all multihulls are born light. A popular cruising cat – a typical representative of modern design – has a displacement of just over 12 tonnes (26,400 lbs) whilst an equally popular monohull of the same LOA weighs in at just under 10 tonnes (22,000 lbs). Both figures are those quoted for light displacement (meaning without crew and stores) so it follows that abusing the catamarans superior stowage capacity could widen that gap still further.

To be fair, in some regards length-for-length comparisons are misleading. In terms of accommodation the catamaran is by far the bigger boat and it's no surprise that it's heavier. It has a larger shell structure, two engines instead of one, and loads of extra furniture and fittings.

But the comparison isn't misleading within the narrow context of performance. To dispense with a keel, only to replace – or exceed – its weight with other items, is to give away the gain made in the first place. At the end of the day, power-weight ratios could decide the winner. And since our two examples have similar sail areas which would it be?

Well, we haven't considered all the factors yet.

Hull shape

All hulls are subject to wave-making drag – a phenomenon that arises from the fact that, as they move through the water, floating objects create waves whose wavelengths – i.e. the distance peak to peak – increase with speed. This is best shown graphically.

This shows the hull at rest with no disturbance to the water

As the boat begins to move forward a small bow wave appears at the forefoot and another wave at the stern

A little faster and a second wave appears forward. Faster still and this wave moves aft until it combines with the stern wave, augmenting its size. The hull is now suspended between bow and stern wave with a trough at mid-length

Naturally, the hull would like to go faster but now faces a serious problem. Any greater speed will increase the wavelength so that the stern wave moves further astern – actually clear of the transom. The after sections of the hull will then sink into the trough and the hull will find itself quite literally sailing uphill. To escape this trap a boat must leave its stern wave behind and climb that hill to get on the plane

The speed at which this occurs is known as the hull speed and can be calculated by the formula:

$$\text{Hull speed (knots)} = 1.34\sqrt{\text{LWL in feet}}$$

Or in metric form:

$$\text{Hull speed (knots)} = 2.43\sqrt{\text{LWL in metres}}$$

We have seen that to exceed hull speed we must summon an extra surge of power to take a boat over the hump into planing mode. But this challenge is much greater for some than it is for others.

It's time to play one of a multihull's strongest cards. Look at the photograph below. A tubby Portuguese fishing boat is shoving aside massive amounts of water and has hit its hull speed well and truly. Its stern is already squatting – that's to say dropping – into the deep trough between bow and stern and a substantial bow wave forms a barrier under its forefoot. No doubt he was late for his supper, for his engine was howling as he passed us in the Ria Formosa – a hopeless waste of fuel in the face of an inescapable restraint.

Now, the opposite of tubby is slender and this is a golden asset for multihulls. Slender hulls disturb the water less, so, while still conforming to the general principle, the waves and troughs they generate are much less pronounced. This means, of course, that they can be surmounted with less effort.

And there's more good news to come but first we should mention Speed/Length Ratios which define where we are in range between zero speed and hull speed – and also beyond should this be possible. The S/L Ratio can be gained by transposing our Hull Speed formula as follows:

$$\text{S/L Ratio} = \frac{\text{Boat speed (knots)}}{\sqrt{\text{LWL (feet)}}} \quad \text{Or metrically:} \quad \text{S/L Ratio} = \frac{\text{Boat speed (knots)}}{\sqrt{\text{LWL (metres)}} \times 1.8}$$

(Actually, the metric world is more likely to use Froude Numbers, but this is a subject beyond the scope of this book.)

Let's take an example to see how S/L Ratios may be applied. Assume a vessel with an LWL of 36ft, moving at 7.5 knots. Therefore:

$$\text{S/L Ratio} = \frac{7.5}{\sqrt{36}}$$

Which gives us an S/L Ratio of 1.25, comfortably below hull speed and actually a nice cruising speed for any boat of this size. But there's more to come.

3

Prismatic coefficients

David Watson Taylor was born in Virginia in 1864 and was to grow up to become one of the US Navy's foremost hydrodynamicists, rising to the rank of Rear Admiral. In 1898 he oversaw the construction of America's first test tank, in which he undertook research that continues to resonate throughout hydrodynamics today. Amongst his many achievements, his work established the important relationship between 'prismatic coefficients' (Cp) and hull drag at various S/L Ratios.

The term prismatic coefficient is misleading, since we usually think of prisms as being triangular in section. What it really means is this: if we were to take the greatest cross sectional area of the hull below the waterline and extend it to equal the length of LWL we would produce a sort of trough shape (see Fig 3:5). The ratio between the volume of the trough and the displaced volume of the hull gives us our Cp which can be thought of either as an indicator of fullness at the ends of a hull or the rate at which the cross sectional area changes.

Due to their inherently tubby shapes, a monohull's rate of change from maximum cross section to bow and stern is relatively and necessarily rapid (see fig 3:5). A typical Cp for a modern design would be in the region of 0.56 (i.e. the hull volume is 56% of the prism volume) which is optimum for an S/L Ratio of about 1.16 – a good compromise intended, as I will now explain, to give reasonable performance over the whole speed range.

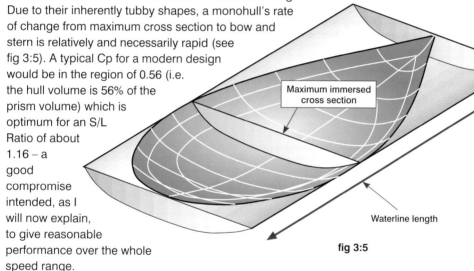

Maximum immersed cross section

Waterline length

fig 3:5

For yacht designers the choice of Cp is a crucial one. This is because Admiral Taylor's research had revealed that, at low S/L Ratios, lower Cps were the most efficient but, as hull speed was approached (or exceeded), higher Cps come into their own. This is great news for multihulls. Since their hulls are narrow, they don't have to make that essential taper towards the bow nearly so early, meaning they can be fuller in the ends without having preposterously bluff bows. As a consequence, a catamaran hull can easily get away with a Cp of about 0.62 – optimum for very nearly hull speed.

The combination of slender hulls and high Cps make multihulls star performers at higher S/L Ratios. Given a decent power/weight ratio (sail area/displacement) they can break through the hull speed barrier with comparative ease, going on to achieve speeds most monohulls can only dream about. The downside is that having a high Cp is a disadvantage at low speeds – another reason why multis aren't exactly sparkling in light winds.

And, talking of winds…

A weather eye on windage

There are more sophisticated methods of estimating wind pressure but Martin's Formula has been with us for decades and yields easily comprehended values by way of a delightfully simple calculation.

So: **$P = 0.004 \times V^2$**

Where:

P = wind pressure (lbs per square ft.)

V = wind velocity (mph.)

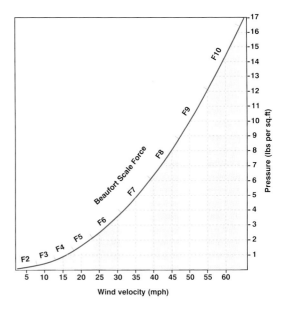

Note that the pressure increases by the square of wind velocity. This means that if the velocity doubles the pressure goes up by four ($2^2 = 4$). A glance at the graph (above) vividly illustrates the point but this, of course, is more than an academic consideration.

All multihulls tend to have lots of windage, most especially catamarans with lofty bridgedeck structures. The action of the wind on all exposed areas will oppose the drive from the sails when beating to windward, will be neutral when reaching, and actually works in our favour when broad reaching or running. The most acute problems arise when the wind pipes up. You can reef your sails, but you can't reef your windage, and you may well reach the stage where all windward progress is denied – not a pretty thought if you're off a lee shore.

Designers have sought to minimise the effects by streamlining their superstructures and keeping them as low as is practicable, but there's a limit to what can be achieved. One of their dilemmas involves a conflicting design consideration.

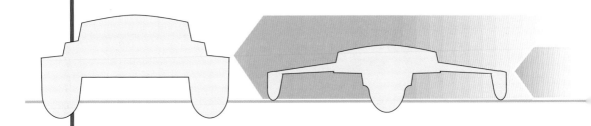

Typical cross sectional shapes for cats and tris. Most catamarans will offer greater windage regardless from which direction it blows

Bridgedeck clearance

Back in the early 1980s I offered to a deliver a 8.2m (27ft) catamaran to the Med. It seemed like a good idea at the time. The summer was exceptionally drear. Work was thin. The thought of escaping south towards the sun for a couple of weeks was irresistible.

In the event it proved a nightmare. At anything much above six knots, the inboard bow waves converged along the centreline, boiling up into a wall of water that totally blocked the bridgedeck tunnel. Our catamaran became a barge, horrible to steer and with a sickening motion. Later, amidst those huge swells so often found near the Berlenga Islands off the Portuguese coast, I nearly flipped the thing end over end as it slewed, virtually out of control, down the slope of a monster wave. It was a scary moment.

The source of its atrocious habits were obvious. The bridgedeck clearance was only 300mm (1ft) at its lowest point and the tunnel was further obstructed by a nacelle that reached down almost to kiss the water. There was simply not enough space for the bow waves to pass through.

One can sympathise with the designer's motives. He was attempting to provide acceptable headroom in a 27 footer – a challenge even in larger cats – without the need for an obtrusive bridgedeck structure and its attendant windage. In the headroom stakes he did quite well, but at a dismal cost to the design's broader role as a sailing vessel. There are no hard and fast rules on bridgedeck clearance but empirical evidence suggests that 700mm (2ft 3in) is the absolute minimum. More would be better, since under bridgedeck slamming is one of a catamaran's less endearing antics.

Compare these two bridgedeck clearances. The cat top right will slam more readily than the one below

Nacelles beneath the bridgedeck can serve several purposes. One confers a foot well along the centreline, thereby increasing headroom in that region and allowing the coachroof to be lowered accordingly. Another reduces the area of zero deadrise (i.e. flatness) to the bridgedeck, softening the effects of any slamming. And a third provides a handy place to fit an auxiliary motor, as we shall discuss in Chapter 7. Unfortunately, the centreline location also places the nacelle where there's the maximum interplay between the bow waves, so the designer might have solved one problem by introducing another. Much depends upon the individual design.

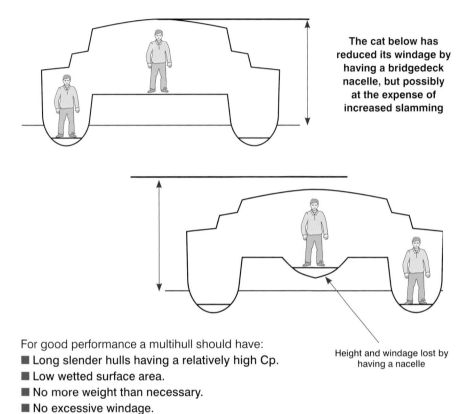

The cat below has reduced its windage by having a bridgedeck nacelle, but possibly at the expense of increased slamming

Height and windage lost by having a nacelle

For good performance a multihull should have:
- Long slender hulls having a relatively high Cp.
- Low wetted surface area.
- No more weight than necessary.
- No excessive windage.
- Generous bridgedeck clearance.

Many of these factors are interactive. Two examples might be:

1. Quite apart from the obvious weight penalty incurred by overloading a boat it will float lower in the water, thereby gaining wetted surface area and reducing bridgedeck clearance.

2. Anticipating an overload, a designer might decide to provide extra displacement by making his hulls fatter only to discover that wave-making drag has increased.

So much for things that might hold us back. It's time to take a look at those that drive us forward.

CHAPTER 4

RIG AND SAILS

'I should have reefed earlier,' a skipper confessed, gazing glumly at the tangle of wire and aluminium that adorned his deck. 'But we were smoking along – having too much fun. The mast buckled just below the spreader. I was such an idiot!'

Our man was being too harsh on himself. Fun is what we are supposed to have. Anyway, it wasn't his fault. It's not too much wind or how much sail you're carrying that causes mast compression failures – *it's the righting moment*. Someone – not the skipper, more likely the designer or builder – had got his sums wrong.

4

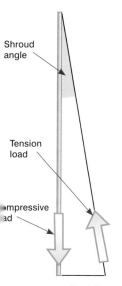

Shroud angle

Tension load

Compressive load

fig 4:1

Let me explain.

Fig 4:1 shows a very basic representation of a stayed rig. A wind force acts on a sail, creating a heeling moment. Since this is opposed by the righting moment imparted by our unseen hull, the windward shroud sustains a tensile load while the mast comes under compression.

What happens if the wind strengthens?

Well, that depends on what type of boat is carrying that rig. Fig 4:2 shows typical righting moment curves for a catamaran (red) and a keelboat (blue). Notice that the keelboat's righting moments build relatively slowly. Pressed by the wind it would heel and, as one might expect, that heeling would increase with wind velocity. Its maximum righting moment occurs at about 60°, by which time the wind would be spilling from the sails.

By contrast our catamaran's maximum righting moment arrives very abruptly at perhaps 15° when the windward hull starts to lift.

Yes, the boat heels a bit at first but there's nothing like the 'reed in the wind' resilience of the monohull. The rig continues to be presented fore-square to the wind force until – whoops! – it's time to ease the sheets.

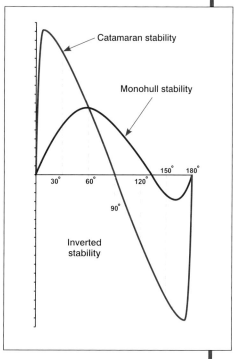

fig 4:2 The curves 'below the line' show the stability when capsized. Note how the cat is just as stable upside down as it is the right way up

The final fact to be gleaned from fig 4:2 (page 25) is that the catamaran's maximum righting moment is approximately twice that of the monohull's. And, since it's mainly the righting moment (there are other factors such as halyard tension and mast weight) that determines what compression loads must be borne, it follows that a multihull is obliged to carry an exceptionally stout stick.

But at least some relief can be gained from a multihull's wide stance.

Fig 4:3 shows our basic rig, but this time the angle between shroud and mast has doubled. Now take a look at fig 4:4 – a graph showing the effects of shroud angles on compression loads. It can be seen that the greater the angle – that's to say, the further outboard the stays are taken – the less will be the compression load. Nearly all multihulls take advantage of this by locating the shroud chainplates as far outboard as possible.

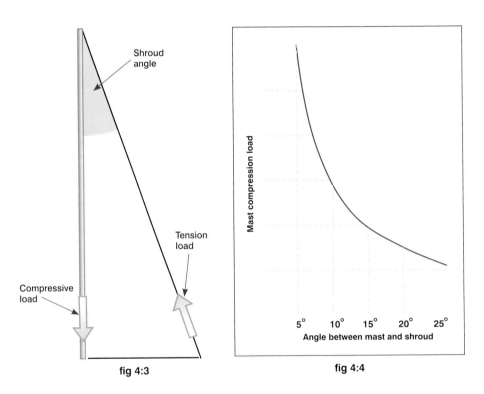

fig 4:3   fig 4:4

Another trick is to stiffen the mast section itself with 'diamond' stays. Fig 4:5 shows a twin spreader rig that provides lots of stiffness athwartships and fig 4:6 an alternative arrangement with single swept spreaders and another strut pointing forward, adding stiffness to the mast in a fore and aft direction. The diamond shapes that give such stays their name can clearly be seen but the important detail to note is that, since they begin and terminate at the mast, in neither case do they contribute anything to the compression loads transmitted to the deck. Only the mast and shrouds and the angle between them have an effect in that regard.

Folding and 'swing-wing' tris usually have their lower shrouds attached to the centre hull to keep the mast upright when in folded mode. Running stays – very often tensioned with simple blocks and tackles – are rigged out to the floats when these are extended (fig 4:7).

RYA Multihull Handbook for cruisers

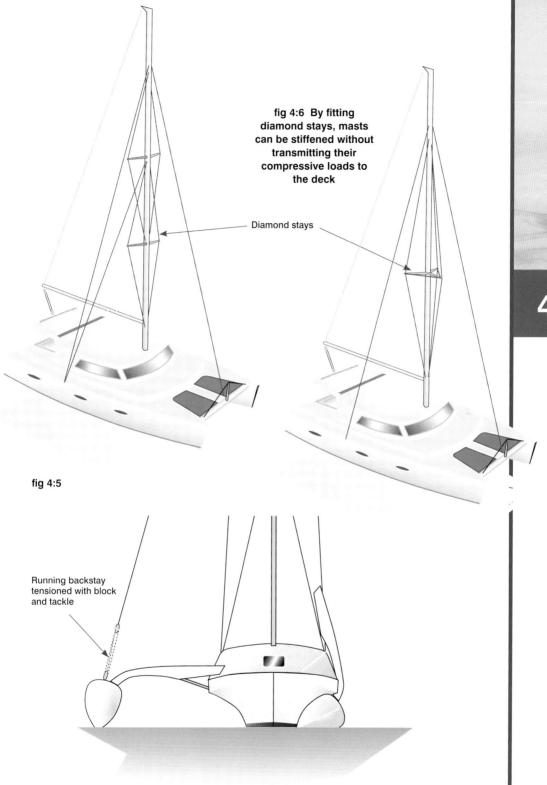

fig 4:6 By fitting diamond stays, masts can be stiffened without transmitting their compressive loads to the deck

Diamond stays

fig 4:5

Running backstay tensioned with block and tackle

fig 4:7 Of whatever type, folding trimarans may need to set running backstays

4

Foils of wind and water

Almost any sails will supply propulsion after a fashion. The very earliest multis have sails woven from palm fronds. But all sailboats benefit from having really good sails – multihulls more than most. To understand why, it helps to take on board some basic theory.

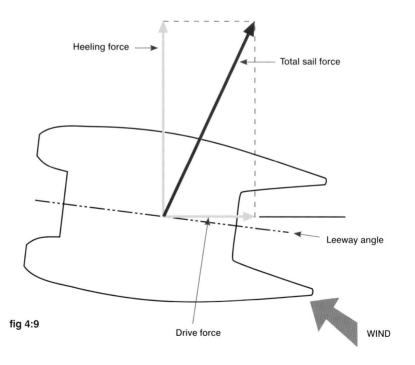

Total sail force

Fig 4:8 shows the forces acting on a sail trimmed for windward work. On the leeward side of the sail there is strong negative pressure in the form of suction, while to windward there is somewhat weaker positive pressure. The summation of these can be expressed as a single line of sail force and the dimension of that force for any given wind velocity depends on the characteristics of the foil shape. This is primarily the responsibility of the sailmaker and, later, the sail trimmer. If the first is incompetent or the sail has stretched beyond usefulness, the second faces an impossible task.

fig 4:8

This sail force can be further split into two component parts: sail heeling force and sail drive force (fig 4:9). You will see that the heeling force vector is much more powerful than the drive force – up to about four times more when beating. This means that the wind is much more intent on blowing a boat sideways (or tipping it over) than it is on driving it forward.

Heeling force

Total sail force

Leeway angle

fig 4:9

Drive force

WIND

Of course, being blown sideways – leeway – is usually undesirable, so what can we do to resist it? Our first defences are the hulls themselves but this is almost always insufficient, particularly with round-bottomed hulls which have less 'grip' than other section shapes. To add further resistance, designers employ various devices:

Fixed fins

Usually of low aspect ratio (see box page 30). Cats have them fitted to both hulls while tris have the options of carrying them on the floats or the centre hull or all three. Although the simplest and most reliable arrangement, fixed fins have their drawbacks: they increase draught; they add permanent wetted surface area; and they can be unhelpful when a capsize risk exists as we shall see in Chapter 8.

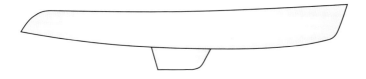

4

Retractable daggerboards

These are almost invariably of high aspect ratio making them extremely efficient. If installed in a trimaran's floats, the foils can be asymmetric like an aircraft's wing, increasing their efficiency. When sailing off the wind or in light airs they can be withdrawn to reduce wetted surface area. However, they are notoriously prone to damage, both from the enormous hydrodynamic forces involved and from grounding or hitting floating debris. By and large the racers' choice.

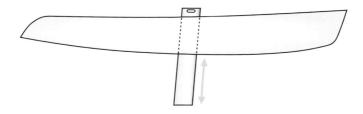

Retractable plates

Rather than being lifted vertically, these pivot upwards when stowed, and can be rigged to do so automatically if they strike anything solid. Typically, they can be operated from the cockpit. Although not as efficient as daggerboards, they represent a very useful compromise for cruising boats.

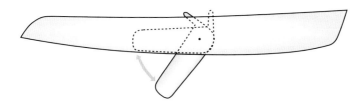

Now let's recall fig 4:9 (page 28) which shows how the aerodynamic forces work. These are opposed by the hydrodynamic forces generated by the hulls and foils, as shown in figure 4:10. It can be seen that the two exactly mirror each other.

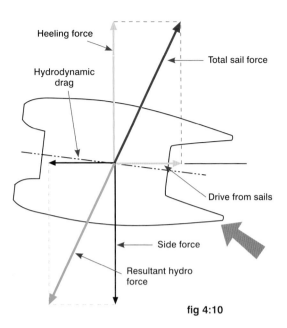

To illustrate their relationships, consider H_{drag} and S_{drive}. In a steady state condition, the two are equal and opposite. Then, along comes a gust of wind and S_{drive} receives a boost. Because drive now exceeds drag, the boat accelerates but, as speed builds drag quickly reasserts itself and the two become equal again at a higher speed. A few seconds later the wind dies back and now it's drag who rules the waves. The boat slows until equality is once more restored – temporarily, for this is an ever-changing situation.

fig 4:10

In this jousting of forces there are goodies and baddies but you can't have one without the other. The objective should be to have efficient aerofoils (sails, of course) working in conjunction with equally efficient hydrofoils (daggerboards or whatever). These are matters where practicalities play a big hand so the perfect solution may well have to be be tempered to suit practical realities.

ASPECT RATIO

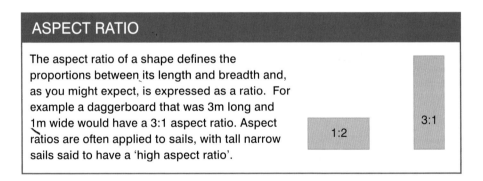

The aspect ratio of a shape defines the proportions between its length and breadth and, as you might expect, is expressed as a ratio. For example a daggerboard that was 3m long and 1m wide would have a 3:1 aspect ratio. Aspect ratios are often applied to sails, with tall narrow sails said to have a 'high aspect ratio'.

Steering

Trimarans usually have one rudder (some racing tris have three!) and catamarans carry two. Because they generally sail faster and more upright than monohulls, rudder blade areas are typically smaller than on their single-hulled counterparts. But, as with all types of boats, control mechanisms range from simple tillers to multi-station steering positions involving complex hydraulics.

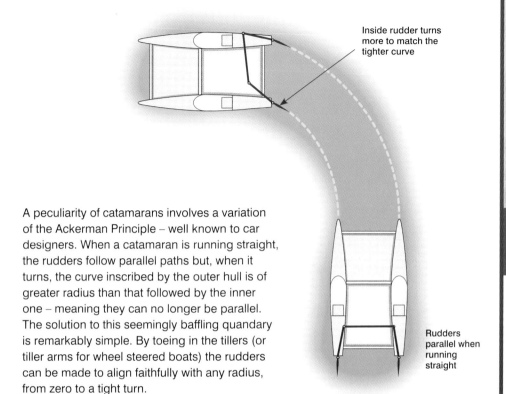

Inside rudder turns more to match the tighter curve

Rudders parallel when running straight

A peculiarity of catamarans involves a variation of the Ackerman Principle – well known to car designers. When a catamaran is running straight, the rudders follow parallel paths but, when it turns, the curve inscribed by the outer hull is of greater radius than that followed by the inner one – meaning they can no longer be parallel. The solution to this seemingly baffling quandary is remarkably simple. By toeing in the tillers (or tiller arms for wheel steered boats) the rudders can be made to align faithfully with any radius, from zero to a tight turn.

The long and the short and the tall

Low aspect ratio rigs – often ketches for larger boats – were very much in fashion during the 1960s and '70s. The reasoning was, that by keeping the centre of effort low, the risk of capsize would be reduced. Actually, squat sailplans perform well off the wind – gaff rigs are exceptionally good – but their performance takes a dive once the wind gets forward of the beam. As you can imagine, planting inefficient rigs on high windage hulls only reinforced the general view that multihulls wouldn't go to windward.

In the Round Britain and Ireland Race of 1974, one of my trimaran designs – *Triple Arrow* – was capsized off the Shetland Islands when, in glass calm conditions, she was hit by a katabatic gust coming off the land. A 21m (70ft) catamaran nearby would also have capsized had not the mainsheet car been ripped off its track. Following this incident, a senior yachting journalist took both myself and the boat to task for the high aspect ratio sails the tri carried. Unfortunately, that eminent commentator failed to notice that, though the sails were indeed of high aspect ratio, the sail area was extremely modest – an attempt on my part to have the sailplan punch above its weight through efficiency rather than brute force.

No need for coyness these days. In the multihull world sophisticated, highly efficient sailplans abound – and rightly so, since there's no point in having all that speed potential without providing the power to achieve it.

Hullo fathead

One advantage of a multihull's wide staying base is that conventional backstays can be dispensed with. This leaves the door open for fully battened mainsails with large roaches – 'fatheads' or 'square tops' in the lyrical lingo of our sailing world. The most obvious and significant benefit these bring is more sail area for any given mast height. Other gains – somewhat more difficult to quantify – arise from aerodynamic principles that were acknowledged way back to the 1930s.

One of the most exquisitely proportioned aircraft ever built was the Spitfire fighter of Battle of Britain fame, renowned for its speed and agility in the air. Its wing planform was in the shape of a modified ellipse, chosen to reduce drag and minimise the wingtip vortexes that occur when the high pressure beneath the wing spills over into the low pressure above it. A lot of birds – the common sparrow among them – also favour elliptical wings, so the shape certainly gets the evolutionary thumb's up. The illustration below shows a Spitfire wing and a modern multihull rig. The similarity between their profiles is marked.

Battens

Given that sails are usually made of relatively floppy materials, mainsail roaches of any size are impossible without supporting battens. Indeed the leeches of non-battened sails are deliberately cut hollow – meaning a negative roach – to put them under enough tension to stop them fluttering. Obviously, battens become even more important where large roaches are concerned, and must be carefully engineered to withstand the compression loads they bear. Most are tapered (in thickness) towards the luff so their bending characteristics match the most desirable camber shape. In this way they bring an additional level of control to sail shape, and with it some worthwhile gains in performance.

Crash gybes are very tough on full length battens. Avoid at all costs by easing the mainsail over in a controlled manner – relatively easily done with the wide span mainsail tracks typically found on multihulls

However, those compression loads bring their own problems. Because they push the luff of the sail forward against the mast, conventional mainsail slides are only practicable on the smallest boats. As you go up in size you rapidly reach the point where batten cars become essential. Naturally, these add weight aloft and their costs can be eye-watering, but they greatly ease the raising and lowering process.

Wear to batten pockets is a perennial problem – particularly at points where the batten might rest against standing rigging. Be wary of cheap sails on which one side of the pocket is formed by the actual sail panel itself. Batten pockets should be made up as separate units which are then attached to the sail and can be removed in their entirety if repair is needed. Sacrificial wear patches should be fitted where appropriate.

Another problem arises if ever a batten breaks – in my experience, not that rare an occurrence. Most are made of pultruded, unidirectional GRP, a material which splits and splinters at the point of fracture into ferocious lances. Expect to shovel extra money in the sailmaker's direction when you buy your new batten.

Expect life with fully battened sails to be somewhat livelier – actually, very much livelier than with soft sails. In terms of acceleration, it's a bit like trading your family saloon for a lusty sports car. Whereas soft sails will flap impotently when feathered to the wind, the fully battened version of the species have a sometimes embarrassing reluctance to stop sailing. To hoist a mainsail at anchor will be to see your boat surging about like a maddened horse straining at its tether.

This type of batten car is designed to run on conventional mast tracks. Larger cars require special tracks - expensive and adding weight aloft

Many years ago, having just competed in the Round Britain Race, I offered to take a landlubberly friend and his young family for a sail in my trimaran. As we rowed out to the mooring my friend impressed on me his eagerness to get involved – don't want to be a mere passenger was his overall gist. Want to get into the thick of it. Glad to hear it, I told him, and proceeded to describe how we would sail off the mooring and how he would be master of the foredeck and have sole responsibility for casting off the mooring line.

Several minutes later we were all ensconced on board, the mainsail raised, and the boat going through its maddened horse routine, sheering from one tack to the other. When I say 'let go', I explained, 'I want you to be quick about it. Take the last turn off the cleat and throw the line and the pill buoy over the side immediately.' He nodded his understanding and marched proudly forward to prepare himself. From my position at the helm I waited until he was ready then, as the mainsail filled on the advantageous tack, bade him let go.

He got the casting off the last turn bit perfectly but, unfortunately, there was something about the words 'over the side' and 'immediately' he had failed to grasp. Instead he turned, eyebrows raised.

'Now?'

That was all it took. Sensing freedom the boat shot off like a rocket. The mooring line went tight, my friend was whisked off the foredeck and his face could be seen goggling at us through the net trampoline as he clattered through the gap between float and hull. Wife shrieked, ditto the children an octave higher, adding a poignant descant entirely devoid of merriment or joy.

It didn't take long to scoop him up again but I believe to this day he blames me for putting him off sailing. He now breeds rare sheep inland somewhere.

WARNING

Be kind to your batten cars and avoid pain to your pocket by preventing your mainsail from flogging. Severe flogging can damage – even destroy – batten cars.

Rotating masts

Another possibility made painless by the wide staying base is the rotating mast. Although very common in dinghy sized cats and dedicated racers, few cruising designs fit them as standard. However, no book on multihulls would be complete without their inclusion.

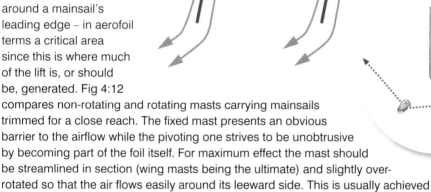

fig 4:12

4

Their purpose is to reduce the turbulence around a mainsail's leading edge – in aerofoil terms a critical area since this is where much of the lift is, or should be, generated. Fig 4:12 compares non-rotating and rotating masts carrying mainsails trimmed for a close reach. The fixed mast presents an obvious barrier to the airflow while the pivoting one strives to be unobtrusive by becoming part of the foil itself. For maximum effect the mast should be streamlined in section (wing masts being the ultimate) and slightly over-rotated so that the air flows easily around its leeward side. This is usually achieved by rigging control lines to a mast spanner protruding forward from its foot (inset).

Although undoubtedly offering advantages, rotating masts also bring their problems:

- Managing the mast rotation is yet another task to deal with every time you tack. And watch out for that mast spanner. It can inflict serious injury if you're standing within its reach.

- In order for a mast to rotate, the shrouds must be attached to a common point on its forward side. This isn't easy to engineer and can cause unwelcome flexure of the shrouds.

- Forget about carrying a tricolour navigation light or a masthead (steaming) light in their usual places on the mast. Some other location must be found. Ditto wind instruments.

- Wing masts are not a serious consideration for cruising boats, since they have a discomforting tendency to create lift even with the mainsail safely bagged below. One skipper I knew had his wing-masted trimaran flip on its moorings and, in a fit of toy-hurling paranoia, alleged sabotage by jealous rivals until calculations showed a recent gale to have been the most likely culprit.

CHAPTER 5

CONSTRUCTION

High speeds produce formidable structural demands. For instance, superficial consideration might lead one to conclude that the side loads on a rudder blade or daggerboard at 10 knots would double if the boat accelerated to 20 knots. Unfortunately, the reality is much harsher. The loads actually increase by the square of the water's inflow velocity – in this case fourfold (i.e. 2^2). This inequitable ramping of loads in relationship to boat speed occurs in many other critical areas.

Naturally, this presents a problem. Since multihulls are – or should be – relatively lightweight structures, the stalwart 'hearts of oak are our ships' approach is obviously inappropriate. To maintain performance without compromising strength, the trick is to build in strength where it matters and save weight in components that are lightly loaded – a principle aerospace engineers would be familiar with.

The choice of materials is crucial.

Timber

Although now completely out of favour in series production circles, timber – mainly in the form of plywood – was the first choice for early multihulls and still remains popular with home and custom builders. And a very fine engineering material it is, too. Strong and easily worked, it's admirably resistant to flexural fatigue – indeed, trees wouldn't stand long if it wasn't.

Despite having fallen out of fashion, plywood remains an excellent structural material

RYA Multihull Handbook for cruisers

Timber's usefulness and durability has been much enhanced by the development of modern adhesives and coatings. So-called 'waterproof' urea-formaldehyde glues were widely used in the middle decades of the last century but their performance over the long term was mediocre. Then came resorcinols followed by epoxies, both bringing their vastly superior attributes to wooden boatbuilding. Epoxy resins also make great protective coatings, sealing timber to a degree never seen before.

As we've already mentioned, the earliest designs were of plywood but dissatisfaction with the slab-sided results soon led to the adoption of more sophisticated methods. Multi-diagonal cold moulded construction, where strips of veneers or thin plywood were laminated over simple formers, became popular and is still in use today.

Growing in popularity is a form of strip planking (fig 5:1), often called cedar strip – a self explanatory phrase where strips of kiln dried red cedar are glued, edge to edge, before sheathing the exterior (and sometimes interior) surfaces with epoxy and glassfibre cloth or rovings. Being light, stiff, dimensionally stable and durable, red cedar is a wonderful material for this purpose. When properly managed, it's also a sustainable resource that should continue to serve us into the future.

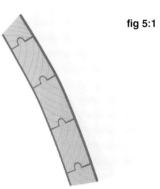

fig 5:1

5

Fibre reinforced plastics

In one form or other, this is the preferred material for the vast majority of production builders. In the UK it's often referred to as GRP (glass reinforced plastic) and in the United States as FRP (fibre reinforced plastic) – the latter being the more versatile description since reinforcements other than glass are becoming increasingly common.

Its strength comes from bringing together two materials offering vastly different properties. The reinforcing fibres are incredibly strong in tension but hopeless in compression. On the other hand, the hardened resin matrix that holds the fibres has little tensile strength but performs well in compression. When the two are combined we have a high strength structural material that can be fashioned into just about any shape we want. Moreover, by adjusting the orientation of the fibres within the laminate, we can choose the axis along which we want the major strength to lie.

Reinforced plastic laminates have their drawbacks. Although very strong, they are also very flexible. Designers often find themselves caught with an excess of strength and a shortfall of rigidity. The answer is usually to fall back on some type of cored construction, a technique that brings huge gains in stiffness with only small increases in weight. Cored construction is widespread in multihull construction, where critical trade-offs between strength, weight and stiffness must be struck.

Glass fibre reinforced polyester laminates endure as the most familiar and least expensive brew, but the stresses imposed by very fast boats are spurring the trend towards more exotic compositions. In the future, expect to see vinylester and epoxy resins used more widely, with high stress areas being reinforced with carbon fibre, aramids (such as Kevlar and Twaron) and other emerging materials.

Foam sandwich construction

Light GRP
laminates both
inside and outside

Closed cell foam
– often PVC

This technique was pioneered in the late 1960s by the British designer and boatbuilder Derek Kelsall. Although labour intensive, it allows custom builders a method of fashioning complex and curvaceous shapes without the need for expensive moulds. The thickness of the double-skinned laminates makes them extremely stiff, making conventional stiffeners such as stringers unnecessary. Both thermal and acoustic insulation is excellent.

- Basically, it involves constructing a simple male jig, corresponding to the internal shape of the hull. This is usually no more than cut-outs of the various hull sections plus longitudinal battens to give support in the intermediate spaces.

- Sheets of closed cell foam (usually PVC) are sprung over the jig and fastened with screws to the battens. Bending the foam sometimes requires heat to soften it temporarily.

- Next, the outer skin of the 'sandwich' is laminated directly on to the foam to the required thickness. Once partially cured, most builders find this is a good time to fill and fair as much of the external surface as possible.

- Next, the hull and jig are rolled over and the jig is dismantled and removed – typically in pieces. The screw heads simply pull through the foam.

- With the hull cradled securely so that it can't deform, the inner skin is laid up on the inside of the foam, completing the sandwich.

Clearly, a great deal of labour is spent filling, fairing and painting, but the time and costs involved are offset by not having to make a conventional female mould.

A foam sandwich catamaran hull awaiting final fairing and painting

CHAPTER 6

HANDLING UNDER SAIL

At the risk of stating the obvious, the word sailing describes the business of harnessing the wind's energy and converting it into propulsion by means of flexible aerofoils we know as sails. Basically, it's not a complicated process. Even a raw beginner can usually get some sort of results from the transaction. But it takes a good deal of understanding and skill to become an accomplished sailor. Alas, all too many find themselves stranded on a sort of ho-hum plateau – good enough to scrape by but never quite excelling. Which is a pity because the fundamentals are easily learned.

This is not a book on the finer points of sail trim but, considering their performance potential, it would be a dereliction not to cover those issues most relevant to cats and tris.

First we must understand the role of our power source – the wind – in all of this.

Winds of change

Let's shelve the complications of sailing for the moment and imagine an open motorboat travelling at 12 knots on a calm day. The crew would feel on their faces a headwind equal to the boat's speed – precisely 12 knots. This, obviously, is entirely due to the boat's forward velocity. Pull back the throttle and all would become calm again. What the crew is experiencing is the simplest form of 'apparent wind' – meaning the wind actually felt by anyone on board.

But what if there's a real breeze – known as the true wind in this context? Surely that happy band in the boat won't feel two distinct winds, one from dead ahead and the other from somewhere else? The answer, of course, is that they won't. The true wind combines with the self-generated headwind to produce an apparent wind that's a blend of them both.

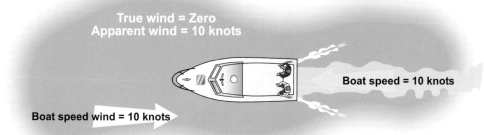

True wind = Zero
Apparent wind = 10 knots

Boat speed = 10 knots

Boat speed wind = 10 knots

fig 6:1

Three further examples will illustrate the point. In the first, the motorboat has the true wind dead astern at 10 knots. Now the boat and the true wind are travelling at the same speed so there will be no velocity differential between them and – as I'm sure you'll have twigged – those on board will feel no apparent wind at all.

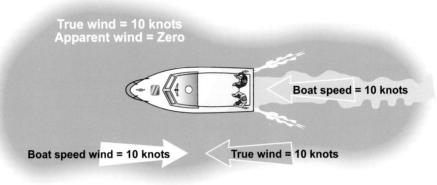

True wind = 10 knots
Apparent wind = Zero

Boat speed = 10 knots

Boat speed wind = 10 knots   True wind = 10 knots

fig 6:2

Now let's look at the opposite situation. The boat turns around and retraces its track, putting that 10 knot true wind plumb on the bow. You would assume that it was going to be draughtier and you would be right, since the velocity differential between wind and boat speed is now 20 knots and that's what the crew will be experiencing. Incidentally, this is why those caught out in heavy weather prefer to run downwind if they can – a subject we shall be returning to in Chapter 8.

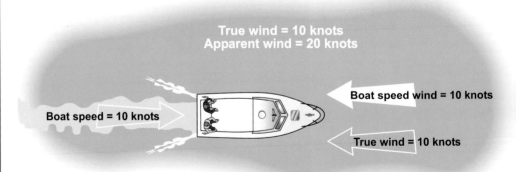

True wind = 10 knots
Apparent wind = 20 knots

Boat speed wind = 10 knots

Boat speed = 10 knots

True wind = 10 knots

fig 6:3

RYA Multihull Handbook for cruisers

But, for now let's concentrate on our third example: the more complex situation where the true wind is anywhere other than along our course line, either ahead or astern. This time it blows square on from abeam. Both boat and wind speed remains at 10 knots.

You've probably realised that, touched on on Page 28, vectors are involved. The drawing below shows how they work in this case, though it's quite easy to anticipate the result. The boat speed component from dead ahead combines with the wind coming from abeam to produce an apparent wind blowing from 45° on the bow. What's more, the strength of the apparent wind can determined by either measuring or calculating the length of the diagonal line – just over 14 knots.

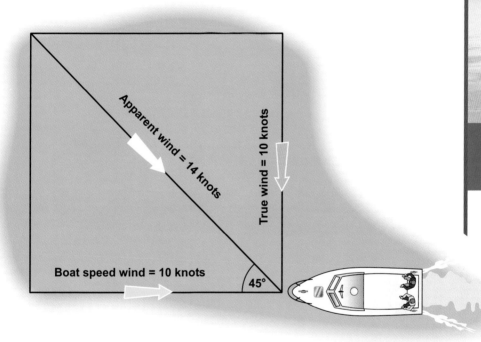

fig 6:4

Velocity made good (VMG)

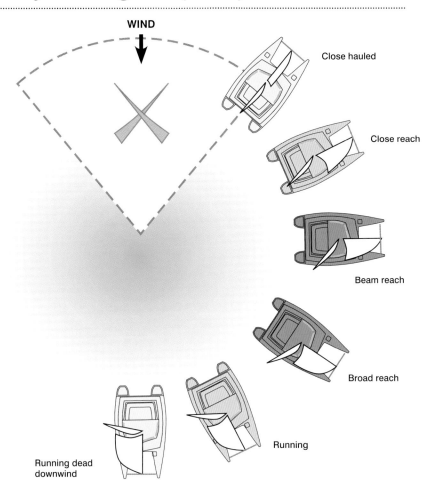

Having outlived its usefulness, we can soon abandon our motorboat and return to the world of sailing. But not before we take another last look at fig 6:2 (page 40) which shows a instance in time when the boat's speed equalled the velocity of the true wind. If we had shown it before it had accelerated to that rate, the apparent wind would have been further aft. Then, perhaps a moment later, the skipper might have opened the throttle a bit, whereupon the apparent wind would have moved forward.

That last sentence is of vital importance to all sailboats which – if you will again forgive me touching on such an obvious detail – can't set a course directly into the wind. Instead they must tack or beat, zigzagging to windward keeping the true wind no more than about 40° on either bow.

For all sailboats, especially fast multihulls, an ironic trap lies in wait. To illustrate the point, I've chosen a high performance multi that, given a good breeze, can sail at twice wind speed. Granted this is a tough call for most cruisers but not impossible for the fleetest brethren and, incidentally, downright pedestrian for ice yachts with their almost frictionless undercarriages.

But we stray. The drawing below shows a trimaran close hauled with the true wind at 40° on the bow. The apparent wind, of course, is further forward – let's say at 27° since this is an efficient boat with well trimmed sails – and has a velocity of nearly 17 knots.

The boat is making about 6 knots through the water but because it must tack, and therefore sails a longer distance, it's only closing its destination at 3.8 knots. This last is known as its 'velocity made good' (VMG) and is the most meaningful indication of a boat's progress.

But the skipper, with a baleful eye on the knotmeter, is becoming frustrated. C'mon, he thinks, this is humiliating for my greyhound of the seas. We've gotta go faster. And he sets about trying to achieve that.

Now here's the rub: he can't – at least not on that heading. The white vectors in Figure 6:5 shows what would happen.

Any increase in speed would cause the apparent wind to move forward whereupon the sails would luff and their drive would be lost. If he wants to sail faster our skipper must bear away from the true wind to maintain that already demanding apparent wind angle.

He takes that option and, to his gratification, the knotmeter edges up a couple of notches. But he's paid a price. Although boat speed has increased, his heading is now further off the course necessary to get him to where he wants to go.

Done in moderation, such tactics can be rewarding. Trading off close-windedness for boat speed can bring useful gains in upwind VMG but it has to be done moderately and in full knowledge of the trade-offs imposed by those vital vectors. Bearing off a few degrees when beating – say, tacking through 95° rather than 80° – will often bring benefits but anything much more than that is unlikely to prove helpful.

But, let's assume our skipper is a total numbskull who believes boat speed will solve all problems. So delighted was he with his first result that he felt emboldened to play the same card again … and again … and, the sad lummox, again.

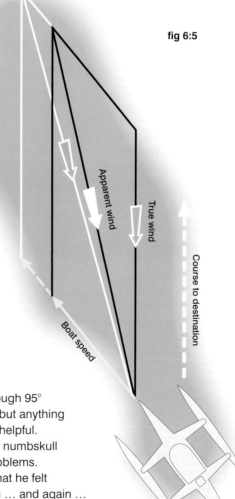

fig 6:5

Apparent wind

True wind

Course to destination

Boat speed

This eventually brought him to the absurd situation illustrated below where the true wind (and his destination) is directly abeam while he remained close hauled, whizzing first one way then the other on reciprocal headings. Boat speed? Nearly 24 knots. VMG? Precisely zero.

Although this is an extreme and somewhat far-fetched tale, it demonstrates how yielding to this sort of temptation is one reason why multihulls have a reputation for poor windward performance. When it comes to losing sight of the real objective, there's nothing like the blood rush of a hissing wake and clouds of spray to deceive and ensnare. A multihull's speed potential can only be exploited when reaching or running. When sailing upwind our supercharged flyer is just another sailboat facing the same dynamic limitations as all other craft.

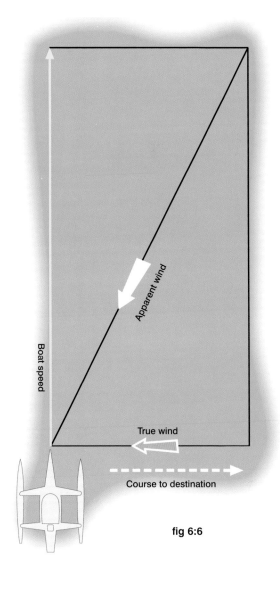

fig 6:6

VMG downwind

On the other hand, when sailing downwind in light to moderate conditions, straying from the rhumb line can be very advantageous, particularly in light conditions. Although most landlubberly types think running is the most desirable point of sail, sailors have learnt otherwise.

Here's why:

■ As we saw back on page 40, when the wind and your course are roughly on the same heading, boat speed is subtracted from the true wind speed, not leaving much in the way of apparent wind to keep sails full and drawing well. For example with a twelve knot breeze from astern, the crew of a boat doing four knots would feel only eight knots. And remember that wind pressure varies with the square of the velocity (see page 22) so the pressure and the work it was capable of doing would drop not by a third but by over 50%.

■ With the wind over the transom, changes to the apparent wind angle are both rapid and erratic. Accidental gybes are a constant threat – bad news for full battens and a sure road to nervous exhaustion. Boom preventers become an almost essential safety feature.

■ Although spinnakers can cope, conventional headsails tend to collapse – even with the wide sheeting options offered by multihulls. Flying the genoa behind the mainsail is a waste of time, since it will be blanketed.

■ Autopilots may not respond quickly enough in such twitchy circumstances. They rely on control algorithms that attempt to 'see' patterns in steering response.

■ Manual steering can be very lifeless and lacking in feel. This is due to the absence of the side loads you normally get on the rudders when reaching or beating.

6

Tacking downwind

Fortunately, you can overcome these problems by tacking downwind. This simple strategy puts the wind unequivocally on one side, thereby vastly reducing the risk of a gybe. It also presents the sails at a more efficient angle to the wind and, what's more, the apparent wind strengthens slightly, further boosting your speed.

I won't bore you with any more vector diagrams but the bottom line is that, if applied to our example from the previous page, putting the wind 20° off a dead run would raise the apparent wind's velocity from 8 knots to 8.3 knots. Hardly earth shattering but useful just the same.

Naturally, this brings up the matter of VMG and you will need to evaluate the situation to see if it's worth it – a simple task, involving some experimentation to see how your boat actually performs in the prevailing conditions.

Let's assume our destination lies due south (180°T) and lies 30 miles away.

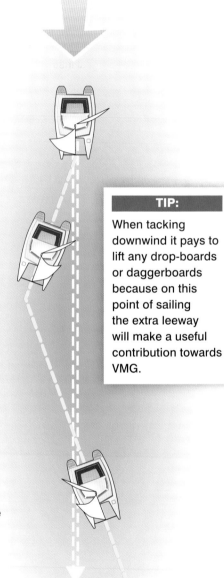

> **TIP:**
>
> When tacking downwind it pays to lift any drop-boards or daggerboards because on this point of sailing the extra leeway will make a useful contribution towards VMG.

- First note the speed you are making on 180° then alter course to 160° (a 20° offset angle) and note the speed again. Let's say that gives us 4 knots and 4.75 knots respectively.

- Now you need to know if that speed gain is enough to compensate for the greater distance you must sail. You could plot this on a chart or piece of paper but it's much easier to use trigonometry. So, we need the equation:

VMG = Boat speed*CosØ

Where VMG is the speed directly towards our destination and Ø is the angle between the rhumb line and the boat's heading.

Therefore:

VMG = 4.75*Cos20 = 4.46 knots

fig 6:7

So, by putting the wind 20° on our port quarter we've gained nearly half a knot of VMG. This would shorten the passage time by three-quarters of an hour and bring with it the extra advantages of extra comfort, ease and safety. What a deal!

Boats with the greatest speed potential will gain the most from tacking downwind – the fastest at even 45° or so to the rhumb line. But it's vital that you keep an eye on that trade-off between boat speed and VMG because, as we saw back on page 44, in the thrill of the chase it's all too easy to lose sight of the principal goal.

As for the practicalities, I use an inexpensive scientific calculator to do the sums but there are simple circular slide rules that will also do the job. Also, some electronic navigational instruments – meaning those systems that interface with each other – can display VMG automatically by computing the interactions between boat speed and the angle and speed of the apparent wind. Whatever tool you use, an understanding of VMG and its implications, both good and bad, is an invaluable accomplishment for all skippers.

In strong wind conditions when you have all the speed you could wish for, tacking downwind becomes a pointless strategy except perhaps to avoid those dreaded gybes – a problem that goes away if you lower the mainsail. More on heavy weather tactics in Chapter 8.

Starting with a reach

A useful trick employed by the lightest craft – particularly those with asymmetric spinnakers – is to gather speed with the true wind beam on, then bear away carrying the apparent wind round with you until you achieve your optimum VMG.

6

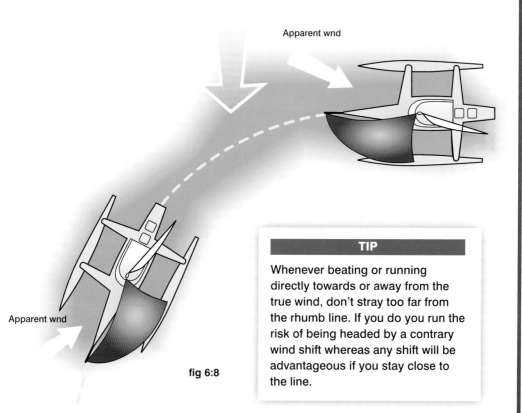

Apparent wnd

Apparent wnd

fig 6:8

TIP
Whenever beating or running directly towards or away from the true wind, don't stray too far from the rhumb line. If you do you run the risk of being headed by a contrary wind shift whereas any shift will be advantageous if you stay close to the line.

Hard as a tack

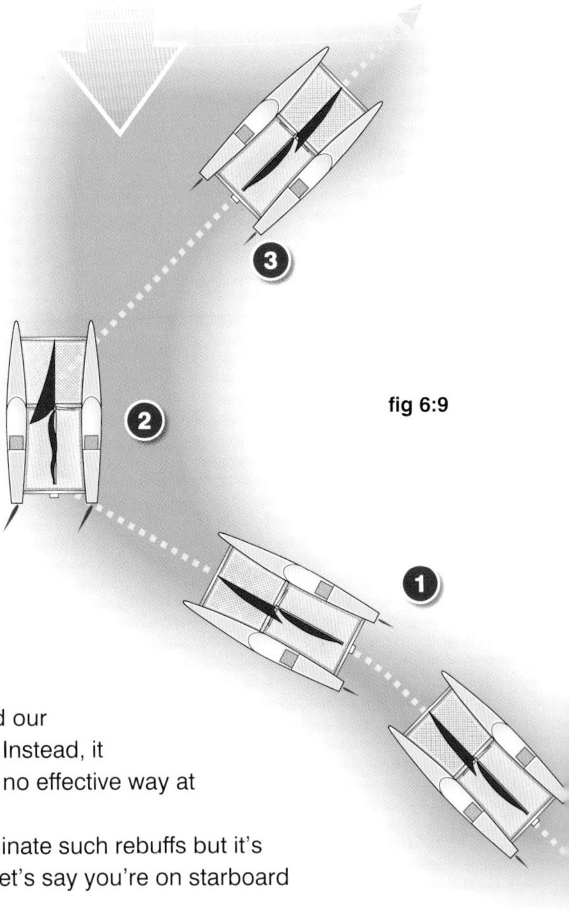

In most regards, handling a multihull under sail is pretty much the same as any other boat – with at least one notable exception. Boats with the sort of directional stability that goes with long slender hulls, more than the average ratio of windage and a lack of momentum arising from light weight, display nothing like the eagerness to tack through the wind as their ballasted cousins.

fig 6:9

The problem is that forward drive is lost at about 40° to the wind, whereupon the boat must carry its way through an arc of at least 80° before that drive is restored. All it takes is for an unfortunately timed wave to slap under its bows and our pirouetting multi pirouettes no further. Instead, it sags helplessly off to leeward making no effective way at all.

There's no way you can totally eliminate such rebuffs but it's certainly possible to minimise them. Let's say you're on starboard tack:

1 As you approach the point where you intend to tack, bear away onto a close reach to gain speed. Then start making your tack when you think you've got enough momentum. Don't creep back to close hauled first. You'll just slow down again. Swing the helm hard over when you're barrelling along. The boat should spin up to windward with alacrity.

2 Leave the headsail sheeted to what had been your lee side – in other words, don't be tempted to haul it across onto the new tack. With the boat now hopefully pointing dead into the wind, the back-winded headsail should now be drawing in such a manner as to push the bows to starboard. You may now be stationary and will soon be blown backwards. If you are – but not before – steer the boat as if going astern, steering the stern to port.

3 Once you have the boat safely on port tack, release the headsail sheet and sheet it in on the starboard side. Mission accomplished!

6

Backing the jib

Leaving the jib sheeted as described is to back the jib. This is a very handy ploy if you ever get caught in irons – that's to say getting stuck head to wind with the sails flapping helplessly. It's also useful when leaving a mooring buoy under sail, allowing you to turn the boat's head in the direction you want to go.

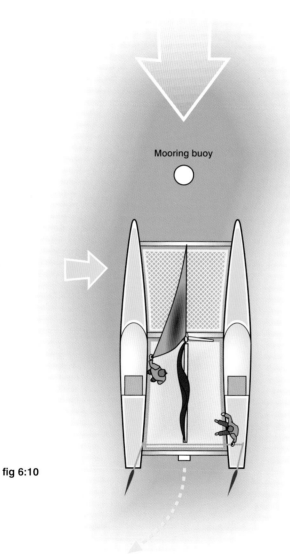

Mooring buoy

fig 6:10

The ideal downwind platform

Witness a keelboat with spinnaker set. Observe the mare's nest of poles and cordage needed to keep it flying. For the crew this is an inescapable necessity, since the sail overhangs far outboard beyond the guardwires, making its control similar in some ways to taming a large unruly puppet.

The fact is that monohulls are wretched beasts downwind. When beating or reaching, the lateral forces in their sails hold them steady. If deprived of these pacifying influences, they can roll abominably. Ask anyone who has done a westbound trade wind passage and watch them shudder. Day after day of dipping first one gunwale then the other is a truly awful experience.

By blessed contrast, multihulls are extremely comfortable in such circumstances. Their natural stability eliminates the most hideous aspects of rolling while their broad spread provide a wealth of places from which to sheet downwind sails – by which I mean spinnakers or twin headsails. And the best news is that this can usually be done without the need for poles.

Twin headsails

This is a great arrangement when the wind is dead astern or nearly so. I once sailed the best part of 5,000nm under such a rig, only very occasionally seeing fit to raise the main.

My trimaran steered itself almost the whole distance. After some experimentation, this was achieved by rigging a pair of sheets to either clew and rigging them as shown below – a system which worked even with the wind up to about 15° or so on the quarter. I started with a single sheet for each headsail, which worked after a fashion but over-steered. Adding a second sheet on each side divided the load between them and dampened the tiller movement. Once set up, I wouldn't touch the tiller for days on end.

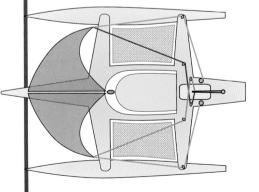

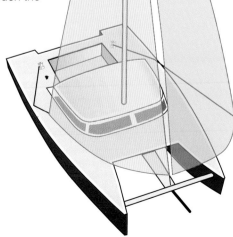

Spinnakers

With the wind more or less dead astern, symmetrical spinnakers work well on multihulls. On that point of sail they can be flown by simply leading their sheets back to the outermost hulls. But they're not the best choice for reaching since they really need a spinnaker pole to function efficiently. However, asymmetric spinnakers – cruising chutes, whatever you like to call them – could have been invented explicitly with multihulls in mind. After all, when there's so much to be gained by broad reaching downwind, who wants the hassles and limitations associated with symmetrical chutes?

Depending on whether you've a tri or a cat, it's possible to fly asymmetrics directly off the bow or forward beam, but a bowsprit or prodder makes life a great deal easier for both types. These can either be fixed or of the portable type that can be rigged when needed, but, either way, they allow the tack to be attached in clear air well ahead of the forestay.

Although they thrive anywhere between a beam and broad reach, asymmetrics are easily blanketed by the mainsail as the apparent wind moves aft. To keep them drawing properly, it helps to pull the tack to windward as shown here.

Asymmetrics can be gybed in much the same way as a genoa by dragging the clew across behind the forestay but, except for in the very lightest conditions, a better method is to allow the sail to blow forward ahead of the boat so it passes ahead of all obstructions. Obviously, you will need extra long sheets to achieve this.

Tack hauled to windward

'Lazy' sheet rigged forward of forestay and tack line

Reefing

You will often hear it said that the time to take a reef is when you first think about it. In other words, it's unwise to procrastinate in the hope that conditions might improve. In the event, if your fears prove groundless you can always shake the reef out again – better by far than waiting till conditions become really hairy.

Since the vast majority of boats carry headsail roller reefing gears, the burden of expertise lies in handling mainsails. On most trimarans this task is very similar to the one facing monohull sailors – but with the added advantage of a steadier platform on which to work. However, catamarans with central superstructures often find boom height a problem, calling for the surefootedness of a mountain goat to negotiate the cabin top. In these cases, some form of remotely controlled system becomes more desirable.

The height of the boom often makes mainsail handling very awkward – particularly, as in this case, if there's a bimini awning as well

---

TIP:

It's the gusts you need to be wary of. Around headlands and in the lee of high terrain, acceleration zones and katabatic winds can arrive suddenly and be extremely fierce. Reef to suit them, not the average wind speed.

We should review the options, starting with the simplest and, in my view, by far the most dependable arrangements.

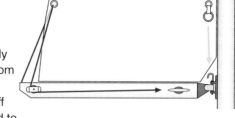

■ **Slab reefing – often called jiffy reefing.** The most basic form involves simple reefing pennants controlling each reef clew. The pennants are usually cleated off to the forward end of the boom but sometimes they're led back to the cockpit. After easing the halyard, the luff of the sail must be pulled down by hand to the point where the reef tack can be secured on the hook just above the gooseneck. Obviously this entails a trip to the mast which some sailors aren't keen on.

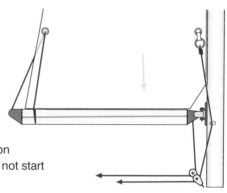

■ **Double line reefing** is a variant of the above. This time a second pennant is attached to the reef tack with both being led back to the cockpit. On the face of it, this looks like an attractive arrangement, but that's only the case if the mainsail comes down smoothly. If not, it's back to the mast as before. This raises the question that if you might have to trot forward, why not start there in the first place?

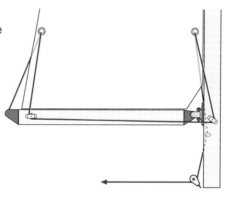

■ **Single line reefing** involves running the reef pennants as shown right. Inevitably, there's quite a lot of friction in the system and the length of the pennants becomes prodigious for deep reefs. This arrangement should probably be limited to smaller craft.

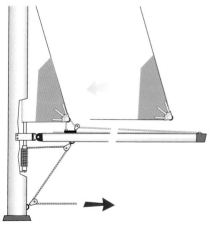

■ Finally, there's **in-mast (or behind the mast) reefing,** where the sail is wound up in much the same manner as a roller reefing foresail. Convenient the arrangement might be, but the risks of the system jamming are significant and, because the foul-up almost invariably occurs inside the mast, they can be exceedingly difficult to clear.

Obviously, conventional horizontally battened sails can't be used, though vertical battens have been developed to work with such gear.

6

CHAPTER 7

HANDLING UNDER POWER

Almost all offshore multihulls are fitted with some form of auxiliary engine, with the choice between the various alternatives depending mainly on the size of the boat. Small multis are often well satisfied with tiny auxiliaries – enough to get them home when the wind falls flat or to help them negotiate the final few yards into their mooring. But this is rarely enough for larger vessels which rely on their engines, not just for propulsion, but also for secondary functions such as electrical generation and the provision of hot water.

The characteristics of engine (either singular or plural) installations and their drive systems has a profound influence on how a boat handles under power.

Let's consider the options:

OUTBOARD MOTORS:
Cheap and cheerful and ideal for the smaller boat, these can either be fixed or steerable, single or double, and can be mounted in various ways – preferably so they can be lifted clear of the water to reduce drag when under sail.

INBOARD ENGINE WITH STEERABLE OUTDRIVE LEG: This arrangement is almost unheard of on trimarans because the engine and drive leg must be situated at the after end of the main hull where their weight would be very disadvantageous. On the other hand, the combination is commonly seen on catamarans, frequently mounted in bridgedeck nacelles on the centreline. The steerable facility is a powerful aid when manoeuvring.

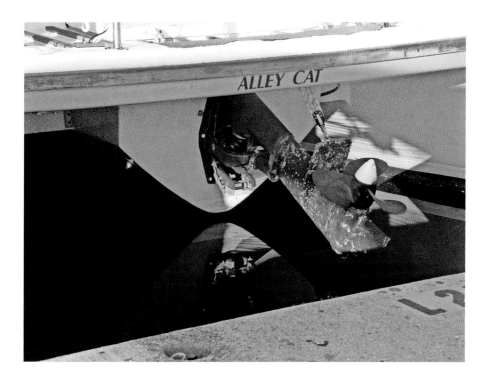

SINGLE INBOARD ENGINE: A popular choice for larger trimarans. The drive can either be via a conventional shaft and propeller or through an all-in-one drive leg unit. Boat handling procedures will be very like those on board a lightweight monohull.

TWIN ENGINES: Far and away the best choice for larger catamarans. Not only do you get the reassuring glow of mechanical redundancy – if one engine fails, the other will get you home – but, as an added bonus, handling becomes superlative. With one engine put ahead and the other astern, the boat can be made to spin in its own length.

7

Thinking things through

Let's face it, multihulls are a bit of a handful in close quarters. Wide, light and usually with loads of windage, they can perform like floating tumbleweed, exacting acute anguish from their skippers – typically in the presence of an enrapt audience, otherwise starved of amusement. It's a fundamental law of boat handling that our worst blunders never seem to occur in private.

All successful manoeuvring depends on thinking ahead and having a clear idea of how the various factors interact. Boats exist in a world of two fluids – water and air – both of which can be moving in any direction over and around those fixed entities represented by the land and all that's attached to it. These include such things as pontoons, dock walls and mooring buoys.

Rudders perform poorly at slow speeds. This, as we know, is because the lift created by foils – and this of course includes rudders – varies with the square of the inflow velocity of the fluid in which they operate. To reduce speed from 4 knots to 2 knots reduces a rudder's effectiveness to a quarter, and at 1 knot to a pitiful one-sixteenth. The practical significance of this is more than academic – particularly for multihulls which, due to their shallow draught and higher top speeds, tend to have comparatively smaller rudders than monohulls. This fact leads us towards the most fundamental rule of boat handling:

> *'If there is any type of current or stream,* **always** *manoeuvre heading into it.'*

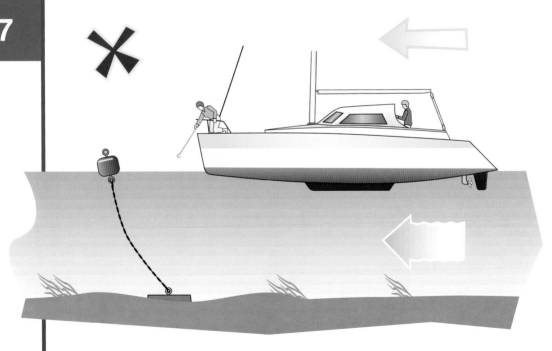

fig 7:1

This simple maxim often seems counter-intuitive to skippers more wary of the mischief caused by wind drift, but the good sense behind it is easily explained. Your controls over speed (engine) and direction (rudder) both lie underwater so it's their relationship with the water that matters. Fig 7:1 shows a catamaran approaching a mooring buoy downstream. The tide runs at 3 knots and the skipper, horrified at the speed of his approach, has knocked the engine out of gear. There is now no waterflow over the rudder blades which means they are useless. The boat is effectively out of control and, if their destination was anything more substantial than a buoy, the outcome could be expensive.

Contrast this with fig 7:2. This time our skipper has done the smart thing and is advancing upstream at about 1 knot. There's now 4 knots of waterflow over the rudders and the boat is fully under control. When they reach the buoy, the skipper simply throttles back a bit, adjusting the speed just enough to stem the tide while the mooring lines are rigged. Simple.

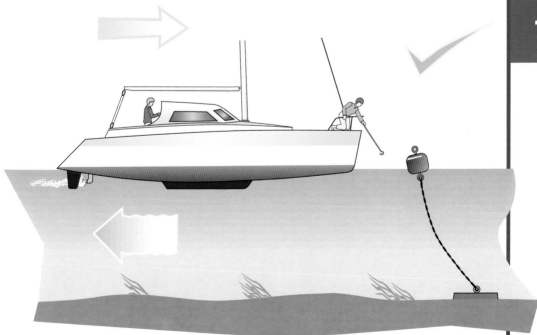

fig 7:2

Dealing with downstream

So, what happens when your destination lies downstream and you have no alternative but to approach it that way? Must you abandon our golden rule?

Absolutely not, since it's vital in all circumstances to maintain your ability to steer. Let's imagine you've arrived at a marina and been assigned a downstream berth. What should you do?

Fig 7:3 shows how. The manoeuvre starts with what's known as a ferry glide – a cunning use of vectors that enables a boat to crab sideways. It's an excellent way of achieving a soft landing in what might at first appear to be tricky circumstances. Used properly, streams are friends not foes.

1 Our skipper makes his approach upstream until he finds himself abeam of the allotted fairway. He then throttles back until his speed through the water is sufficient to stem the tide.

2 Next, he applies a bit of starboard helm, just enough to turn the boat to put the stream on his port bow.

3 The boat will now start to crab sideways to starboard and he will now find it necessary to play the throttles to prevent the boat either dropping back or creeping ahead.

4 When he reaches a point immediately upstream of his berth, be straightens the boat up and eases the throttles. The boat starts to fall back under full control until it's properly positioned alongside the pontoon. Job done.

So, to recap:

'Never surrender your ability to steer. Lose steering and you lose control.'

7

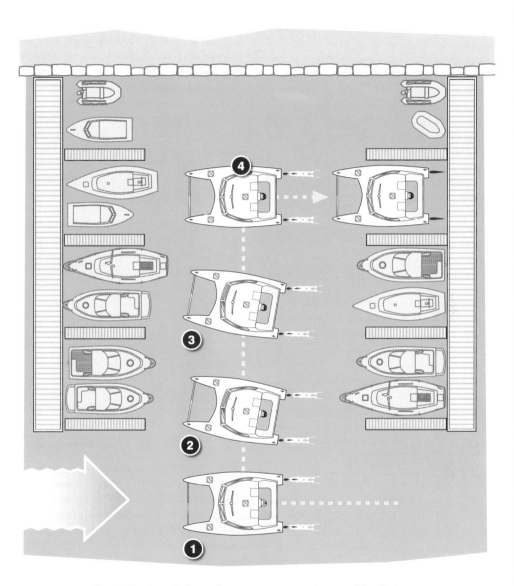

fig 7:3 Far from being a threat, a stream can be your friend when manoeuvring in close quarters. To be able to travel sideways is an immense boon in such circumstances

7

Coming alongside

In the absence of any stream, leeward berths rarely present problems. You simply manoeuvre yourself to a position close to the berth and the wind will blow you on and keep you there. You will find yourself enjoying the luxury of having plenty of time to nip ashore and secure the mooring lines.

Windward berths are less considerate. Unless you are very brisk in getting crew ashore, the wind will carry you away as soon as you stop, perhaps even leaving the crew stranded.

The solution is to rig a mid-ship spring – a useful berthing aid in a wide variety of situations and almost indispensable when coming alongside a windward berth.

The sequence as shown in fig 7:4.

1 Attach a short mooring line to a cleat at about mid-length with a pre-made loop in the other end. A crew member should carry the loop forward towards the inshore bow. Once ready, make your approach at about 2 knots making sure the bow doesn't get blown downwind.

2 Reduce speed as you approach the end of the finger. As soon as he is able, the crew member steps or jumps onto the finger and immediately drops the loop over its outermost cleat. Depending upon the freeboard, he may even be able to do this without leaving the boat.

3 The helm then reapplies a bit of thrust and waits for the spring to pull taut. When it does he steers the stern in towards the finger. The boat is now completely under control and can be left to its own devices while you set about completing the mooring. The stronger the wind, the greater the power needed to hold the boat alongside.

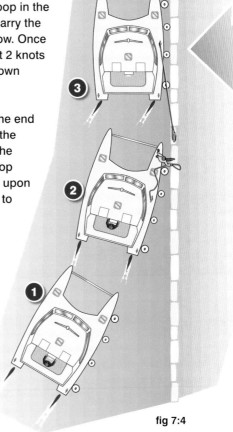

fig 7:4

Since you only need two people to manage a mid-ship spring, they're a godsend for cruising couples. The technique can be adapted for all sorts of circumstances and is the 'default' method on many boats. If you haven't got a suitably positioned cleat, fit one. I can assure you you'll never regret it.

7

More on springs

Leeward berths are a cinch to get into but departure can be a tougher proposition. Fortunately, this is another situation where springs can get you out of trouble.

If there's no stream you can 'spring off' either the bow or the stern, the choice being simply a matter of whichever suits you best. However, if there is a stream, you should spring off the upstream end to take advantage of its effect. Fig 7:5 shows a cat springing her bow off and it can be clearly seen how the stream helps the boat rotate.

The sequence unfolds like this:

1 Single up your mooring lines to just a bow and stern line and rig a stern slip line spring. Place a large fender on the port quarter.

2 Once all is prepared, engage reverse power and take in the stern line. As the tension comes on the spring, the stern will swing towards the wall.

3 When you are ready to leave, increase the reverse power and let go the bow line. The bow will pull clear of the wall, and the stream (if there is any) will act on the hulls to swing them out further.

4 Everything OK? Then engage neutral, slip the spring and motor clear. Make sure the spring doesn't foul the prop.

The procedure is exactly the same going out stern first but, of course, the various actions are reversed.

7

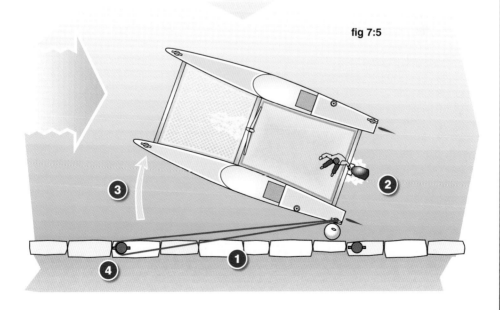

fig 7:5

Board drill

Multihulls with retractable kick-up boards or daggerboards can use them to advantage. Multihulls with fixed fins are stuck with what they've got.

Although all skippers know that their boards will help reduce leeway when beating and create unwanted drag when running, it's not always fully appreciated how they affect the way a boat manoeuvres under power.

Fig 7:6 shows how a catamaran might behave when (a) the boards are down and (b) when they are up – both at the same speed and with the same degree of helm applied. Example (b) will make a wider turn than (a) because there is less lateral resistance to counter the centrifugal forces induced by momentum.

Either characteristic could be useful in certain circumstances but, as a general rule for close quarters manoeuvring, we should leave the boards down in windy conditions and lift them up when the wind is light.

Of course, twin screw craft can tighten their turns by throttling or putting into neutral whichever engine is on the inside of the turn. Indeed, they can turn in their own length by putting one engine ahead and the other astern – a tremendous asset where space is tight.

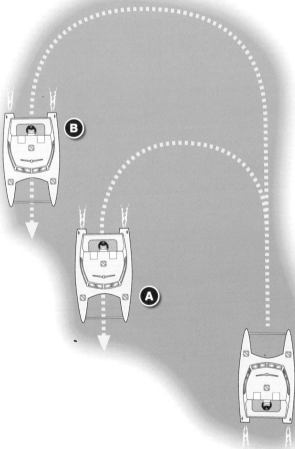

fig 7:6

Anchoring

When it comes to dropping the hook, multihulls have distinct advantages. Due to their shallow draught, they can anchor nearer inshore, where they will often find better shelter – in non-tidal waters perhaps conveniently within wading distance of a beach. This is just as well, since they rarely carry all-chain rodes, preferring a chain and rope combination to save weight.

A keelboat might lay out a length of chain equal to three to four times the depth of water and, in moderate conditions, will stay fairly close to its anchor thanks to the heavy chain's catenary. On the other hand, the multi with a rode made up of a few metres of chain and the rest of rope will need at least six times the depth and will stretch that to near its maximum in anything approaching a stiff breeze. Shallow water means the necessity for a shorter rode, hence a smaller swinging circle.

In truth this segregation due to draught is helpful to both types. Whereas keelboats will almost invariably lie to whatever stream might be running, multihulls tend to sheer about at the mercy of the wind (see below). This means that the spaces between boats can change radically when the tide turns, converting what at first might have seemed a sensible spread into one where they could easily come together.

Wind over tide

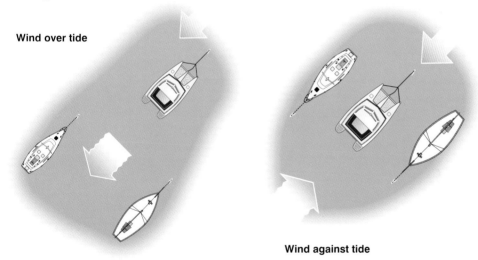

Wind against tide

Laying out a pair of anchors can limit the swing but this is a messy arrangement where the chances of snarl-ups are high. An alternative arrangement in a reasonable depth of water is to stream a drogue (see page 72) from the stern so your boat lies to the stream.

If the wind is chaotic in direction – a common occurrence in anchorages where hills can cause eddying effects – another problem arises. When there are frequent changes in direction an anchor can be snatched out and, before it has had time to dig in again, the multi will have blown several dozen metres downwind. This can happen to any boat, of course, but multihulls are notoriously frisky when anchored and will drift faster and further if they are unlucky enough to lift the pick. Make sure you pay out enough cable.

Bridles

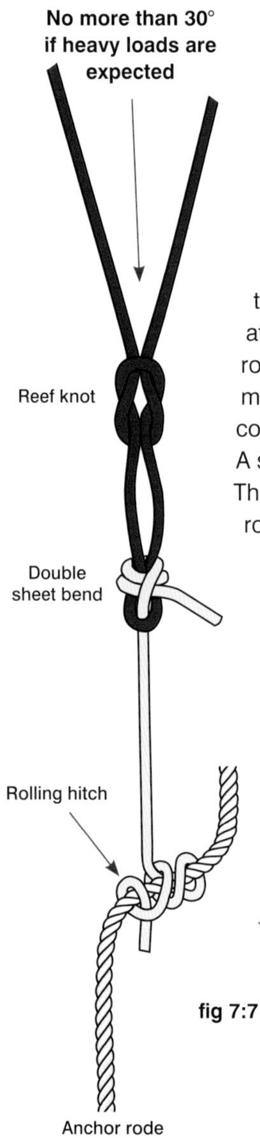

No more than 30° if heavy loads are expected

Reef knot

Double sheet bend

Rolling hitch

fig 7:7

Anchor rode

As you might expect, trimarans range their anchors directly off their main hull bow exactly like monohulls. Catamarans must use some sort of fairlead on their forward beam but this can be unsatisfactory if the beam is set far aft of the bows. For them the answer is a bridle which, as we shall see in the heavy weather section starting on page 67, can also be used for streaming a drogue from the stern.

The bridle is basically 'Y' shaped with two long arms that are secured to the bows and a much shorter 'tail' that's attached to the rode. It should be made up of stretchy nylon rope. There are many ways bridles can be assembled but my own preference is shown in fig 7:7. The two arms are a continuous length with a reef knot creating a loop at mid-length. A short tail is then bent to the loop with a double sheet bend. The tail should be attached to the rode with a rolling hitch. If the rode is entirely of chain, a chain hook could be used but, again, a rolling hitch would serve.

Don't make the arms too short or there will be severe lateral loads attempting to pull the bows inwards. For the arms, an included angle of about 30° is about right.

It's important to make sure all securing cleats are up to the job, with generous backing pads on the underside of the deck. Light weight and stoutness don't always go together, and I know of several boats whose cleats have pulled out, taking part of the deck with them. In very rough conditions consider leading some back-up lines aft to the sheet winches.

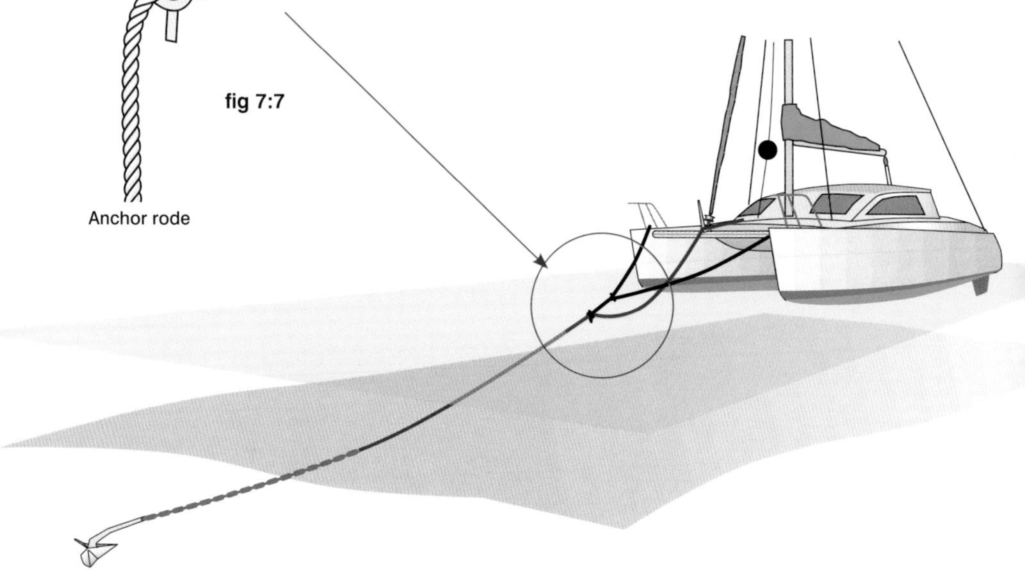

Alongside a tidal wall

Catamarans have few problems lying alongside quay walls but trimarans with dihedral cross beams are another matter. Their natural rocking motion means that their shoreside floats constantly scrape up and down, perversely dislodging the fenders placed there as protection. At least that latter problem can be overcome by running a line under and around the float (see fig 7:8) but the relationship between boat and wall will always be somewhat uneasy.

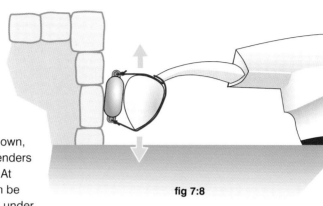

fig 7:8

Whatever the type, provision must be made for the rise and fall of the tide. The short breast ropes you might use at bow and stern in non-tidal waters or against a floating pontoon clearly won't do because they will plainly leave you dangling at low water. The solution is to use an arrangement as shown in fig 7:9, with bow and stern lines extended along the wall – a good rule of thumb being that their length should be at least three times that of the tidal range. Bow and stern springs should be rigged similarly.

7

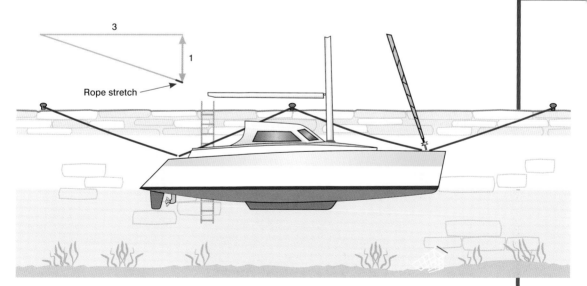

3

1

Rope stretch

fig 7:9

Rafting up

'Catamarans make convenient fenders,' a monohull skipper once told me. 'Their sides are nearly straight and they have lots of freeboard. No chance of getting the gunwales hooked under my rubbing strake.' We were talking of rafting up, an increasingly common experience in the most popular destinations. So, if you own a cat, expect lots of company on your overnight stays. The social potential is vast but you may need some defensive precautions.

The most important ingredients when rafting are courtesy and consideration from all involved. Here are some pointers:

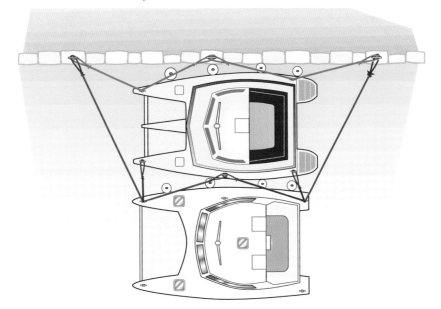

- Try and raft against a boat of similar size, certainly not one much smaller than yourself.

- If there's anyone on board, ask permission before coming alongside. He may be planning an early start when you're looking forward to a lie in. If that's the case you have no right to impede his departure and will be obliged to rouse yourself.

- If the boat is unmanned and you plan to go ashore, leave a note with some contact details: supping a pint at the Throttled Frog or your mobile phone number.

- Even if there are fenders waiting to receive you, deploy your own, and plenty of them.

- Don't depend on someone else's shore lines. Run your own lines ashore after you have secured to the host boat.

- Respect the other's privacy by crossing via the foredeck. Don't invade his cockpit unless invited to do so.

CHAPTER 8

HEAVY WEATHER TACTICS

By far the best defence against the most ferocious meteorological antics is to avoid them if at all possible. Unfortunately those weasel words 'if at all possible', are a necessary caveat for there is never absolute certainty about the weather. There's no doubt that modern forecasting techniques have improved greatly but they are still not 100% reliable, as a couple of tragic events testify.

In the 1979 Fastnet Race, 17 competitors lost their lives when an approaching gale suddenly intensified. And then, in June 1994, a fleet of over 80 yachts – many participating in a rally to Tonga – left New Zealand in conditions that were thought to be improving, only to sail into what's known down under as the 'Queen's Birthday Day storm'. One boat disappeared entirely with the loss of three lives. A number of maydays were issued and the crews of 9 boats rescued.

Of significance to us is that we know that amongst that antipodean fleet there were at least three catamarans. One endured the storm and emerged relatively unscathed and another was sunk deliberately at request of the owners – once, I should add, they were safely aboard a rescue vessel. The couple crewing the third cat – a home-built 38 footer called *Ramtha* (designed by my brother Roger Simpson, incidentally) – was also taken off and the boat was later salvaged, afloat and intact, after the storm had abated. The same happened in the '79 Fastnet when several boats were abandoned and then recovered afterwards.

Given good fortune and a modicum of common sense, most sailors are unlikely to face such appalling conditions. In over 50 years of sailing, I can only remember one occasion when I was thought I was in serious peril, though there have been innumerable times when it's been thoroughly unpleasant and I had wished I were somewhere else.

It's important not to underestimate the effects of bad weather on crew morale. Fatigue and discomfort can easily make things seem much bleaker than they actually are and can soon dispirit a crew. On an extended ocean race before the days when wind instruments were common, researchers asked skippers to estimate wind strength as they went along. Almost to a man they reckoned the wind stronger than it actually was, indicating a tendency to believe things were bleaker than they actually were. Not for nothing is a Force 6 known as a yachtsman's gale because that's what it feels like to most of us.

8

> **TIP:**
> The onset of a storm is not the time to first make friends with your storm canvas. Get the sails out of their bags and hoist them in calmer conditions to familiarise yourself with their workings and ensure that tack strops are of the right length. If temporary sheet blocks are required, make sure they are available and you know exactly where and how they must be attached.

Heavy weather sails

Moderate increases in wind strength can be coped with by reefing but there's a limit to the benefits you can gain. The problems arise from one of the basic tenets of sail control: to power up a sail you introduce fullness; to de-power it you should make it flatter. So, when the wind pipes up, the last thing you want are the baggy sails that usually come with reefing.

To be fair, slab reefed mainsails can often achieve quite acceptable shapes but you can't expect the same from furling headsails. Once you start to roll the sail, the luff tension relaxes and the sail bellies hopelessly. There are various ways of mitigating this effect – padded luffs to take in some of the excess fullness for example – but these only help for the first few rolls. So we are left with the irony that the stronger the wind, the more deeply we must reef and the progressively fuller and more unsuitable become our sails.

Modern roller reefing has made misers of us all. Unlike the days when boats carried a selection of headsails, each matched in area and cloth weight to suit a narrowish range of wind strengths, we now expect just a mainsail and genoa to serve us through everything from near calms to howling gales. This is unreasonable. And a false economy. Modern sailcloths are undoubtedly strong, but you only need to stretch a fabric just once beyond its yield point for it to be ruined forever. The abused sail will never return to its original form making it even less suited to heavy weather sailing than it was before.

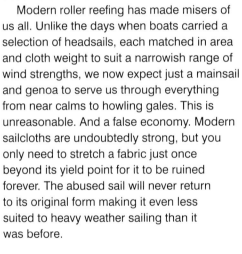

Storm jib set on detachable inner forestay

Trysail sheeted independently of the boom

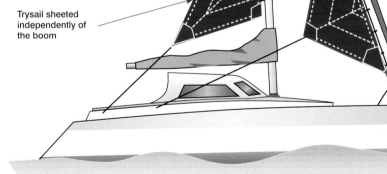

fig 8:1

8

And here I should put in a plea for buying good quality sails. Cheap sailcloths are usually loosely woven and employ resin fillers to help them maintain their shape. They are very much more likely to be ruined by overstress than top notch sails.

A coastal skipper may get away with the basic inventory of main and genoa but the serious offshore sailor should consider dedicated heavy weather sails – namely, a trysail and storm jib (see fig 8:1).

The trysail is a surprisingly useful sail and, for many purposes, a much better alternative than taking a third reef in the mainsail. If you have a fully battened main with sophisticated batten cars, the trysail should run up on its own track, thus bypassing the main track entirely. Even if you don't have batten cars a separate track is a good idea. It should

A dedicated trysail track means the sail can be hanked on at deck level

run down to almost deck level so the slides can be inserted in relative safety. Trysails are usually sheeted independently of the boom, allowing the latter to be secure amidships where it can't swing about and injure anyone.

There are various methods of setting storm jibs, the most convenient of which is to hank it on to an inner forestay, either permanently rigged or portable. It's important to choose the system that best suits your boat.

Uphill battles

Many years ago I was delivering a heavy displacement keelboat to the Mediterranean. We had rounded Cape St Vincent and were halfway to Gibraltar when the Levanter struck. With a wind gusting over 50 knots and very large seas, we plugged away for the better part of a day – motor-sailing for the last hours until we ran low on fuel. In the end we gave up and ran back to Villamoura on Portugal's southern coast. We learned later that a French yacht had gone down in the vicinity, prompting a vain search for survivors.

My reason for relating this story is to show that not even a yacht with low freeboard and the punch of substantial tonnage (and, as we learned in our case, no storm sails!) can make meaningful upwind progress in such conditions. A light displacement monohull would have fared even worse and a high windage multihull – a typical cruising cat, for instance – would have thrown in the towel earlier still. Remember, you can reef your sails but you can't reef your superstructure. There comes a time when the windage wins.

Hopefully, you will never confront such extremes, but the chances of getting caught in awkward but still sailable conditions is pretty high. You will find that a useful trick is to luff up slightly as you breast each wave (see fig 8:2) then bear away to gather speed ready to tackle the next one. This takes skill because it's all too easy to get caught in irons, so it's certainly not a task you should entrust to a novice or an autopilot.

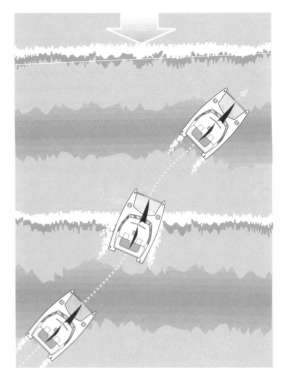

fig 8:2

But the sea is a capricious environment and fortune doesn't favour us all. Despite our best plans and precautions, there's always the chance that one day we will be confronted by something really nasty. Motor sailing can extend your upwind abilities – a potential lifesaver if pinned off a lee shore – but, when wind and sea state make further progress impracticable, most skippers will take the seamanlike decision to turn tail and run downwind – assuming they have the sea room, that is.

> **CAUTION!** It's impossible to overemphasise the care that must be taken in gusty conditions. Reduce sail before it becomes absolutely necessary and moderate your speed. The wise skipper always assumes the worst and takes the necessary precautions to minimise the risks.

Downwind dangers

In comfort terms, the contrast between beating and running is to step through a portal from misery to relative luxury. As if by magic the apparent wind speed drops – and typically drops a lot for a fast multihull – and there's an almost instantaneous end to the drenching spray and all that bone-jarring pounding that threatened to loosen your teeth. The sense of relief can be overwhelming but it's time to be wary. The welcome respite can mask a threat.

For now our enemy is boat speed. This is usually regarded as an asset but an excess of it can be dangerous when you find yourself accelerating down a watery ski-slope at over 20 knots.

But there's more to waves than just an alternating series of obliging ups and adverse downs. It's the actions within them we should watch out for. Anyone who has helmed in following seas will recognise the forward surge you get as a wave crest passes under you, and then the lurching sensation that occurs as you sink into the trough.

They could be forgiven for thinking that this is simply the contrast between the start of a downhill slide followed by the prospect of an uphill grunt, but that's far from being the whole story. What's not always appreciated is that there's an orbital action within each wave, and that the surface water moves in different directions depending on where you are on the wave face.

Fig 8:3 shows a simplified representation of the way waves work. Think of a single water molecule on the rim of an imaginary wheel. As the wheel rolls forward, the direction and strength of the surface flow changes. Now we should imagine a boat sailing downwind – that's to say from left to right in the diagram. It's blowing hard enough for the boat to sail faster than the wave train. Let's examine what may happen step by step.

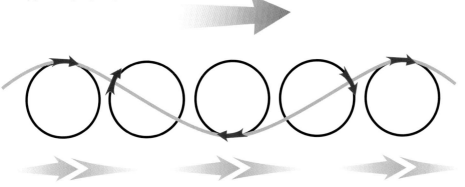

**fig 8:3 The red arrows show the direction of the surface flow.
The green arrows below show variations in the flow's speed**

- When our boat reaches a crest, the surface flow adds to its speed and gives it a playful flick into the void beyond. This is the surge we relished earlier.
- For a brief moment the steering becomes less effective as the inflow velocity over the rudder blade is reduced. The timing is unfortunate to say the least since this is the time we should be squaring up the boat for the exciting bit to come.
- Now boosted by gravity, the boat surfs joyfully down the slope gathering speed as it goes, then …
- … when it reaches the trough it encounters the surface water rushing up to meet it – our braking effect.
- This is the moment of peril. Half the boat still wants to accelerate while the bows are balked by the counter flow. It's a bit like slamming on the front brakes of a bicycle. If a bow digs in, the whole shebang could slew round and … oops! … the classic pitchpole or diagonal capsize.

In reality, waves are less orderly. The harder the wind blows, the steeper they become – the more pointy their peaks and flatter their troughs. And, more often than not, there are probably different wave systems, generated from outside your immediate area, superimposed over each other to make a nonsense of simple mathematical models. In very heavy conditions – say F9 and above – the sea state can become extremely chaotic, with no discernible pattern to the waves at all.

But, for now, let's assume the wind is fierce but not horrific. We need to tame its effects.

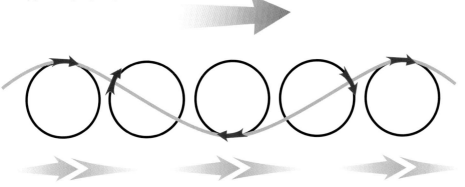8

Drogues and other drag devices

Clearly, if too much speed represents a danger it must be moderated. Your first step should be to reef. Start with the mainsail, lowering it entirely if necessary. When running in heavy weather it's safer to be towed from the head rather than pushed from the stern, which can slew you round. So, should conditions permit, try and leave a scrap of headsail set to maintain steering control, but there may come a time when you're forced to reduce to bare poles.

A Galerider drogue which forms an elliptical shaped basket when towed astern

If your downwind speed remains excessive you should consider towing a drogue – a drag-creating device specifically intended to act as a brake. There are various proprietary models on the market. If properly proportioned to match your boat they can have a remarkably soothing effect, quelling the headlong rush and stabilising your steering by keeping you orientated more or less stern to wind. Ironically, there's a danger in going too slowly and, in doing so, increasing the impact of the advancing waves. It's all a matter of judgement. You may find the best combination is to run with a small headsail set and a drogue astern.

In the absence of readymade drogues, they can be improvised. One or more bights of rope have been suggested, as have old motor tyres trailed astern. All might work, though their efficacy is impossible to foretell. As with storm canvas, it pays to try these out in milder circumstances before you need them in earnest.

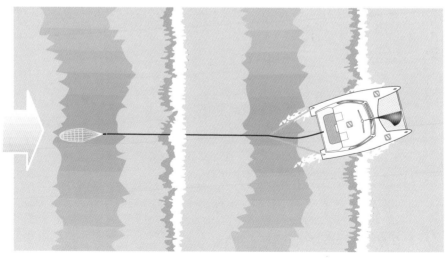

fig 8:4 Bridles can be rigged asymmetrically to allow the boat to run a little off dead downwind

The tow line should be of nylon to take advantage of the material's elasticity. Choose eight-plait or braided construction since three strand rope has a tendency to unwind under load, causing the drogue to rotate. It can be attached to the stern at a single point but a better arrangement is to use the anchor bridle as described on page 64. Make sure all cleats are strong enough and any fairleads are well padded to prevent chafe.

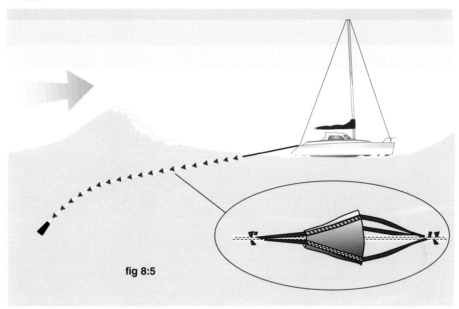

fig 8:5

Applying drag to the stern gives a boat a natural tendency to sail dead downwind or at a slight angle with the wind on a quarter. It also helps hold the stern down, at least partially suppressing any delinquent inclinations to broach or pitchpole. Except with series drogues (fig 8:5) the distance astern is critical. Drogues should be positioned about a wavelength and a half behind the boat so, as you surf down a wave face, it is being pulled through solid water where it's unlikely to pop out of the wave face (fig 8.6). Clearly your tow line must be long enough to allow this and the length should be adjusted accordingly. I carry 100m which doubles as a spare or kedge anchor rode.

Finally, lift all boards. The ability to skid sideways is a useful defence against capsize.

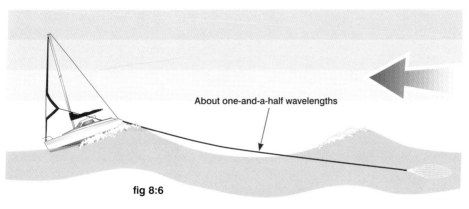

About one-and-a-half wavelengths

fig 8:6

Reaching in the rough

It's not just times of obvious peril that are hazardous. When it's howling Force something-we-hoped-never-to-face, and the air is filled with spray, there's no doubt where our thoughts are focused. Survival is the only preoccupation. Less easy to read are those in-between circumstances when life is lively enough to whip up the adrenalin but not scary enough for the alarm bells to peal.

One example is when beam reaching in a fast multihull – about as thrilling an experience as you can have under sail. It's very easy to push a boat to its maximum stability – that's to say when the hull – (or hulls for a tri) are about to fly. With any further heeling the stability tails off rapidly, as you can see from the stability curve on page 25. To add to the risk, the waves are coming at you from abeam, perfectly placed to give the windward hull an unhelpful upward boost.

Of course, as always the best precaution is the practice of good seamanship. Here are a few points to bear in mind:

■ First the obvious: get the crew weight to windward.

■ Make sure all sheets are free to run if you need to ease them in a hurry. Remember that mainsheets typically run through multiple blocks so are particularly prone to foul-ups. Use the least possible turns around winches and, if they are self-tailers, pass the unloaded tail back behind the winch so a single jerk will release it (fig 8:7). Alternatively, ignore the self-tailing facility and use cam cleats instead.

fig 8:7

fig 8:8

fig 8:9

■ Flake rather than coil the excess rope (fig 8:8).

■ If you need to use boards at all, use the windward one, keeping the leeward board raised. That way the boat has a chance to slip sideways if the windward hull lifts. (fig 8:9)

■ Bear away if overpressed and needing to de-power fast. On no account round up. The combination of an increase in apparent wind and centrifugal forces acting on the rig could be the last straw that flips you over.

■ But, above all, never be reluctant to reef. Don't be the skipper, sitting astride a hull, who wished he had done so earlier. Match your sail area to the gusts, not the milder interludes in between.

8

RYA Multihull Handbook for cruisers

Sea anchors

The terms sea anchor and drogue are often used interchangeably but actually don't describe the same sort of device. Drogues are almost always towed astern and are intended to reduce boat speed and increase directional stability. By contrast, sea anchors are streamed from the bow and are designed to hold a boat more or less head to wind, though of course some slippage will mean it will inevitably drift very slowly astern. Some monohull sailors – particularly skippers of heavier displacement craft – advocate using bridles so their boats lie at an angle to the wind, but this is not recommended for multihulls which are safer taking the wind and seas from dead ahead rather than having them crash obliquely onto their relatively fragile topsides.

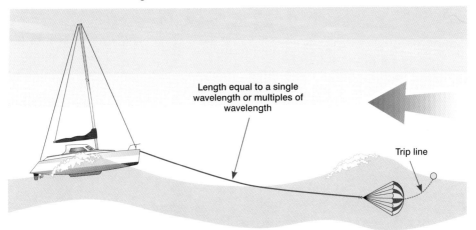

Length equal to a single wavelength or multiples of wavelength

Trip line

fig 8:10 Boat and sea anchor should be in the same part of their respective waves so they rise and fall at the same time

The truth is that there's a general lack or hard data on sea anchors, though one reliable – though some might think unlikely – source are commercial fishermen (particularly in the US and the Antipodes) who use them to stay on station over their fishing grounds in bad weather or overnight. For yachts, much of the information is anecdotal and many of the oft-quoted incidents took place in rough but not extreme conditions with assumptions being extrapolated from the lessons learned. It's also the case that an arrangement that might work well for one boat could prove unsatisfactory on another. Since personal experimentation is impracticable, boat owners must weigh up what evidence there is and choose the approach that makes the most sense to them.

By far the most popular type are parachute anchors, similar to those used in aviation. Indeed, many have been adapted from precisely that source, though there are now a number of companies producing dedicated marine versions, with the term para-anchor often being used to describe them.

Since the object is to effectively anchor the boat in position – bar some slight and unavoidable drift – it follows that the para-anchor must be capable of holding a weight of water sufficient to achieve this. A common mistake is to carry too small a chute. The recommended size for a 12m (40 ft) multihull, for example, would be about 4.5m (15ft) diameter and it's always better to err on the big side if in doubt.

Jackstays and harnesses

The fact that multihulls sail without excessive heeling is a huge boon to anyone working on deck but can create a false sense of security. In lively conditions and at all times at night, crew should wear safety harnesses and be tethered, either to jackstays or to fixed clipping points in the cockpit.

The purpose of a harness and tether is not to tow you astern like a harpooned whale but to stop you going over the side in the first place. This means the jackstays should run well inboard of the boat's perimeter and not along the side decks as you so often see. The exact routes will, of course, depend on the boat itself and it's almost certain that some compromises must be made. There's no reason why you should not have more than one set of jackstays – perhaps along the cabin top to work the mast and another set to restrain you forward.

The good sense behind harnesses, tethers and jackstays is obvious but there's a particularly grim peril that rears its ugly head if you capsize. Those lifesaving tethers of a length designed to save you falling overboard could also prevent you swimming out from under an inverted hull.

Therefore tethers should have clips at the harness end that can be released under load. And, as a backup:

■ **Anyone wearing a harness should also be equipped with a knife. This is never a bad idea on a multihull, anyway.** Crew have perished trapped beneath trampolines.

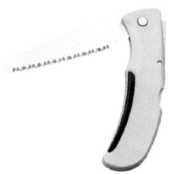

Heaving to

It's debatable whether this manoeuvre belongs in a chapter on heavy weather because its usefulness spans a wide range of conditions from light through moderate to at least moderately heavy. Beyond that – and particularly if the seas are breaking and could crash down upon you – it could indeed be dangerous. No matter. Heaving to deserves a place somewhere so here it is.

As experienced sailors will attest, there comes a time when it's important to draw breath – perhaps to make repairs, prepare a meal, or simply take time out to put your feet up. Heaving to is the marine equivalent of pulling your car into a lay-by and resting for a while.

Not all boats behave the same when hove to. Much depends on the underwater shape and how the windage is distributed. But most lightweight craft will lie at about 35° to 55° to the wind and will drift slowly down a track about 45° off dead downwind.

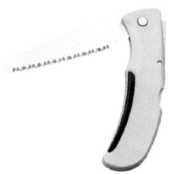

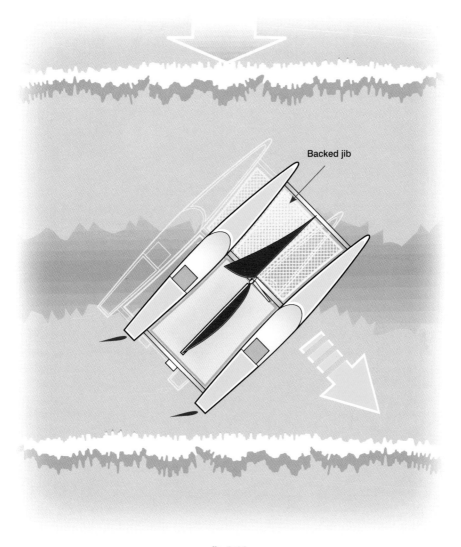

Backed jib

fig 8:11

Fig 8:11 shows how it's done. The headsail is backed to windward and the mainsail – deep reefed if conditions demand – is sheeted more or less amidships. The helm should be lashed hard over as if wanting to steer upwind. Alternatively, you can tack through the wind (page 48) leaving your headsail aback once you've done so.

When hove to you need as much lateral resistance as possible so, in anything less than very heavy weather, all keels or boards should be lowered. In more extreme conditions (and for the reason discussed in the next section) only the windward board should be down.

As you might have guessed, heaving to is another tactic that should be practised first. No one can predict exactly what combinations of sail area, trim and rudder position will work the best.

Experiment, experiment, experiment!

CHAPTER 9

COPING WITH CAPSIZE

The do-it-yourself righting of capsized multihulls has attracted a lot of thought and talk over the years. Some ideas have been ingenious and some downright potty. All are impracticable without outside help. Asked how he might set about it, a crusty singlehander once remarked: 'That's what cranes were invented for.' In my opinion he was right.

Anyway, most of us sail in waters where help is usually close to hand. And the backdrop has changed in other ways. When that extraordinarily accomplished and gentlemanly American sailor, Phil Weld, flipped his 18m (60ft) trimaran *Gulf Streamer* en route across the Atlantic to the UK for the 1976 OSTAR, he and his crewman were obliged to occupy the inverted boat for five days before being taken off by a British container ship. Despite having three radio beacons on board they were ignored by numerous over-flying aircraft and saw several ships while they awaited rescue.

Since then, of course, communication technology has advanced enormously. Back in the 1970s, VHF radios were quite primitive. They presented a considerable drain on batteries and were expensive enough to deter many from buying them. Unsurprisingly, relatively few small vessels carried them so, with fewer people listening, 'mayday' transmissions could easily go unheard. Now it's rare to find a boat without at least one VHF radio on board.

Then, for those venturing far enough offshore to be out of VHF range, there are 'Emergency Position Indicating Radio Beacons' (EPIRBs). Early models transmitted on a frequency of 121.5KHz and should be considered obsolete. They can no longer be relied upon. The latest EPIRBs operate on 406MHz (or both 406MHz and 121.5KHz – the latter being retained for homing purposes) and allow satellites to identify your position anywhere on the globe. Those with built in GPS will pinpoint your position to within a few metres.

All of which is good news for sailors. Although nothing can ever be assured, should you be unfortunate enough to capsize there is now a very good chance that your distress calls will get through and that someone will come to your assistance.

9

Will she float?

This might seem a ridiculous question but it isn't something that can always be taken for granted. We know that multihulls don't have ballast keels and that many multihulls are built of buoyant materials – timber or foam-cored laminates being common, but that doesn't automatically mean they will stay afloat. And there are also those constructed of single-skin GRP or even aluminium.

What must be remembered is that even the most inherently buoyant multis contain notable sinkers such as engines, mast and rigging, various items of metalwork along with all the other bits and pieces that go to make up the whole. To evaluate the entire structure, setting one item against another in terms of buoyancy, would be a nightmarish task that would almost certainly to lead to little more than an approximation.

Better by far to build in more than enough flotation in the form of enclosed compartments. Trimarans with fully sealed floats (and sometimes cross beams) score easily in this regard but catamarans usually require positive action at the design stage. Popular sites for buoyancy compartments are at the ends of the hulls and beneath bunks.

The need to provide buoyancy has widespread formal recognition. For example, in their race rules for offshore multihulls the International Sailing Federation (ISAF) specify that 'adequate watertight bulkheads' be fitted to render the boat 'effectively unsinkable'. Another provision calls for a watertight 'crash bulkhead' within 15% of the bow. Although both of these stipulations are primarily concerned with holing rather than capsize, clearly there are benefits for the crew either way up.

And ISAF are not alone. Other interested bodies are similarly insistent on the subject.

9

Anticipating the worst

It's tempting to think that, by making a boat unsinkable, you eliminate the need for a liferaft. But this would be rash since no boat is truly unsinkable as long as it can catch fire. Also, to be run down by a ship could reduce it to matchwood – most of it floating but none of it of much use.

However, the oft-quoted axiom that you should only abandon your ship as the very last resort is still as valid as ever. If you can make it tenable, your inverted multihull is the safest survival capsule you have, being more visible from the air, much less prone to wind drift and carrying more useful gear and provisions than you could ever transfer to a liferaft.

Here again the various authorities more or less sing as one, specifying safety measures that increase in stringency with boat size (and therefore likely usage) and, in some cases, year of manufacture in recognition that older vessels can't always be adapted.

Of particular note are:

(A) Each habitable space should have an escape hatch, capable of being used in the capsized position and of a size through which a fully clothed person can pass (450mm aperture diameter being a recognised minimum). The hatch should also be capable of being opened from both inside and outside.
Catamarans will have their hatches fitted in the inboard sides of their hulls so that escaping crew will emerge onto the comparative safety of the bridgedeck. Tris of over 12m (39ft 5in) built 2003 and later should have two hatches.

(B) There should be enough handhold and clipping points on the underside for all crew members to secure themselves. On tris these should be around the central hull. Pre-rigged jackstays running under the bridgedeck are another good idea – insisted upon by some offshore racing bodies.

Although not necessarily specified, other sensible preparations would be:

(C) Non-slip surfaces to critical areas that might be walked on when – immediately outside the escape hatches, for instance.

(D) Fluorescent orange paint over a significant part of the inverted surface. For tris with no side decks the underside of the beams would be ideal.

(E) A small watertight locker, accessible from the underside containing a torch, knife and – possibly for boats without escape hatches – the tools for cutting same. Exactly where to cut should be determined (and preferably marked) beforehand.

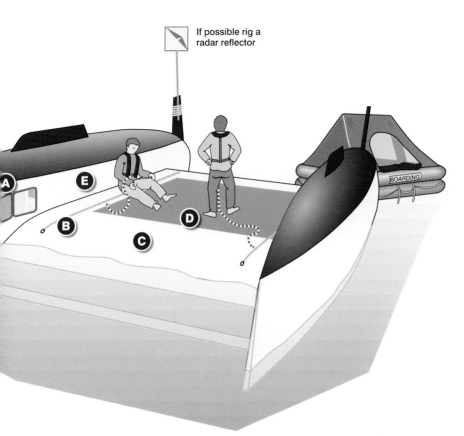

If possible rig a
radar reflector

BOARDING

For reasons that are obvious, monohull
sailors are familiar with substance flying
off shelves and learn early that everything
must be well secured. The same can't be
said of many multihullers who are lulled
by their upright experiences to fancy that
everything will stay where it is regardless.
Not in a capsize they won't.

And here I'm not thinking of the odd
broken plate. Ask any yacht surveyor how
often he finds such items as batteries
and gas cylinders that might be laterally

**The liferaft should be stowed where
it can be reached from the inverted
position**

chocked in place but not strapped down to resist capsize. When surveying
multihulls, he will tell you, they are almost always found to be inadequately secured.
Yet it takes little imagination to picture the damage or injury such objects could
cause if they became projectiles. And such apparently benign objects such as
carpets can be lethal. Think how difficult it might be to crawl out from under one if it
descended to enshroud you. They shouldn't be just sitting loose on the cabin sole.
Fit restraints of some kind – press-studs or similar.

Capsize!

The worst has happened. During a momentary lapse in concentration an awkward wave lifted the windward stern and caused the lee bow to bury. Over she went. The prudent skipper would have thought about this calamitous event in advance and discussed and planned for it with his crew. Hopefully all on board would know what to do. Their plan should go something like this:

1. Immediately check that all the crew are safe, and that none are trapped under or inside the hull or have been thrown into the water. The boat won't be carried away by the wind so any MOBs won't be far away. If anyone is missing and not in evidence in the water, tap the hull where they might be trapped inside – a responding signal would be a very good sign. Hopefully there's an escape hatch that would soon enable them to join you outside.

2. With all the crew safe, make sure they are wearing a lifejacket with correctly adjusted harness and securely clipped on. Capsizes usually occur in rough conditions so things could be tough with plenty of wave action.

3. Put out whatever distress signals are appropriate without delay. If there are other vessels nearby these would include:

   ■ A 'Mayday' call on VHF. If your radio has a GMDSS facility, activate that as well. However, it's likely that your main VHF radio is probably out of action. Even if the radio itself is still above water, the antenna almost certainly isn't. At only 5W output, a handheld radio's range is much more limited.

   ■ Activate your EPIRB if you have one (see page 78).

   ■ Let off flares (most effective by night) or orange smoke during the day.

   ■ There's no harm in alerting someone using a mobile phone (assuming it survived the dunking) but remember that rescue services can't home in on it in the same way they can with other forms of radio transmission, though they can identify the general area. Preferably phone someone who will understand your predicament and can relay your position accurately. Remember, maritime jargon can mean nothing to landlubbers.

If further offshore, the VHF Mayday call and GMDSS are still worth a go but a 406MHz EPIRB offers the best chance of summoning help. Activate it immediately.

■ **RYA Sea Survival Handbook (G43)** offers invaluable further reading. www.rya.org.uk/shop

WARNING:
Be very careful diving down to under the boat. It might be very tempting to go looking for useful gear stowed there but remember the tangle of ropes, sails and even anchor chain that could ensnare you. Do not attempt it if there is any wave action.

Life on the flip side

If help is unlikely to be imminent you will need to settle in for the duration – however long that might be. Prepare for the worst. Try and imagine ahead of time how your world would change if it suddenly turned upside down. Think about the resources available to you and how you should use them.

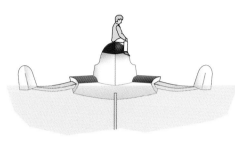

Capsized multihulls will not all float at the same level. Various factors will determine the end result: the disposition of buoyancy compartments and entrapped air being the most significant. But we can hazard a guess. Fig 9:1 gives some idea how the various types might float. It can be seen that trimarans with dihedral crossbeams would probably end up with their centre hulls carried high enough to provide reasonable shelter. Faring rather worse are flatter tris and catamarans which will float lower. As you might have surmised, cats with bridgedeck structures will have their saloons totally immersed.

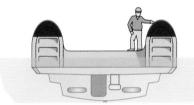

fig 9:1

Here are some useful precautions, the first harking back to the previous section:

- Spilled battery acid will make a bad situation worse. Fit sealed batteries (preferably gel cell type or AGM). And strap them down. Since they are usually fitted in locations that keep their weight low, they should be clear of the water after the boat flips, thereby conserving a very useful resource. The same could be said of anchoring portable tanks, water containers and toolboxes but perhaps that's asking too much.

- Being tipped out of their stowage isn't the only way you could lose gear. With the boat half flooded there will be a powerful surge action as the water swills back and forth. It's important to make sure that vital items such as EPIRBs, handheld radios, torches et cetera, can be stowed where they can't easily be dislodged, and located where they can be retrieved when capsized.

- It's also useful to think about how you would exist in this inverted universe. Think comfort – though, in this context, this is a somewhat relative term. However, maintaining morale is important, for which an important commodity is sleep. And here you will face a problem. Obviously, one of the first things you lose are those once cosy bunks, now directly underneath. Acrylic canvas hammocks (with drain holes so they won't collect water) and somewhere to sling them should be an early priority. They are compact to stow and quick and easy to rig.

9

Emergency 'grab bag'

The purpose of a grab bag is to assemble in a handy container – usually a canvas bag in high visibility yellow – a selection of useful items you can take with you to assist in your survival. What you should include will depend largely on the specific challenges you will face. For example:

1. Where you are sailing. If it's a coastal trip your chances of attracting attention and being rescued soon are good. A mobile phone could be of huge importance, with water and particularly food being a lesser consideration. In the middle of the ocean the reverse applies.

2. The prevailing climate and season. In higher latitudes keeping warm is of utmost important whereas sunburn could be the principle enemy in the tropics.

3. Your action following the calamity. An intention to abandon ship – fire! – will make some items vital. Colonising the upturned hull to await rescue will suggest other priorities. Remember that liferafts contain survival packs already containing some items – their contents vary so check what's included.

Multihull skippers should take stock of where their priorities lie and make their choices accordingly. The following list makes some suggestions.

Suggested contents of a grab bag

- Orange smoke flares
- Signalling mirror
- EPIRB
- Handheld VHF (waterproof)
- GPS
- Mobile phone
- Torches (waterproof)
- Mini binoculars
- Water
- Food
- Serrated knife
- Multitool
- Flippers and mask

- Fishing line
- Space blanket
- Protective clothing
- Sunscreen
- First aid kit
- Seasick pills
- Personal medication
- Spectacles
- Sunglasses
- Passports
- Money & credit cards
- Ship's papers

9

RYA Multihull Handbook for cruisers

Man overboard

There's no doubt that to lose a person over the side is one of the scariest things that can happen at sea. This is a MAJOR EMERGENCY that requires immediate attention – especially on a fast multihull which might sail a considerable distance before being brought under control and able to return.

The first reactions to the emergency should be:

- The first person seeing the person going into the water should shout MAN OVERBOARD to alert the rest of the crew.

- Someone should be detailed to keep the casualty in sight at all times, preferably pointing at the MOB with an outstretched arm.

- Throw the Danbuoy (and its strobe) into the water to help provide visual reference.

- Someone should press the MOB button on the GPS or chart plotter and, if available, the 'distress' button on a DSC type radio. A voice message can wait for a minute or two or, if there's a handheld VHF, send a Mayday alert from the cockpit.

These actions should take no more than a few seconds, even if shorthanded. It's now time to recover the casualty, for which there is no single procedure that fits all occasions. Much depends upon the circumstances at the time.

Unless you have no alternative, don't attempt to recover the MOB under sail. Use the sails to stop the boat then return to the casualty under motor.

As an example, let's take a cat on a beam reach.

9

1 The casualty is fishing off the stern and falls off.

2 Immediately he becomes aware of the problem, the skipper (assuming he isn't the MOB!) takes over the helm and turns the boat through the wind, whereupon the boat becomes effectively close hauled. He starts the engine.

3 Next, the headsail is furled or dropped – but not the main. Instead, the mainsail is sheeted hard amidships to reduce its drive and stop it swinging about.

4 The skipper then drives the boat at 90° to the wind to a position just upwind of the MOB, using reverse and forward thrust to allow the boat to drift down onto the MOB, who is then recovered from the leeward side.

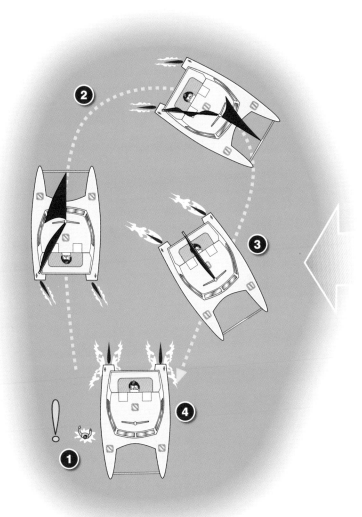

If you have no option but to recover the casualty under sail, you should use the classic figure-of-eight recovery procedure.

This time we have our boat beating to windward when the crew goes overboard. So:

1 The skipper bears away onto a beam reach as soon as he becomes aware of the emergency. He then prepares the crew to tack, telling them they must furl or drop the headsail as they pass through the wind.

2 Once through the wind, the skipper puts the boat on a broad reach.

3 The final approach is made close-hauled under main alone to a position upwind of the casualty. Once there, the mainsail is eased completely and the boat drifts downwind towards the MOB.

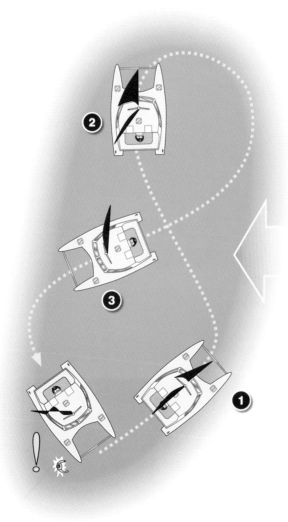

The use of trampolines is very common on multihulls and there is much to recommend them. Usually of webbing or open netting, they are light, offer very little windage and are easily grabable should you lose your footing. But they are also potentially treacherous.

Back in March 1983, the eminent offshore sailor Rob James was lost from his trimaran *Colt Cars* when a chafed trampoline lashing let go, dumping him into the cold spring waters of the English Channel.

Routine inspection of lashings and netting is essential. Always remember the deteriorating effects of UV light and never use polypropylene netting – commonly used for fish nets – because it is particularly susceptible to UV degradation.

Polypropylene netting degrades quickly in sunlight. This example was spotted on a Greek day charter catamaran – not exactly an encouraging sight

9

Harnesses and lifejackets

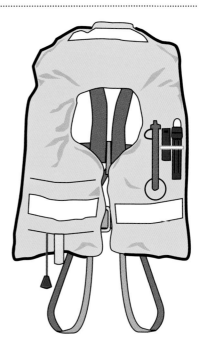

Of course, the best precaution is to do your utmost to prevent it happening in the first place. This means harnesses and lifejackets should be available for those working on deck. Fortunately, these are usually combined in a single, comfortable unit as shown above.

The tether should have safety clips of approved type, designed not to unclip accidentally. See page 76 for more on this subject.

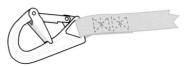

150N is the most appropriate lifejacket.

Whether tethered or not, lifejackets should always be worn in the following circumstances:

■ In an open boat such as a yacht tender.

■ At all times by children on deck.

■ At all times by non-swimmers at any risk of entering the water.

■ On deck at night or in rough conditions.

■ Whenever the skipper decides it's necessary. If in doubt, wear one.

9

NOTE: Multihull race rules demand that inflatable lifejackets should be gas inflated – a sensible requirement. But there is some concern regarding the automatic inflation type which, it is argued, might prevent you swimming clear if you were trapped under a capsized boat or trampoline. The same argument applies to foam filled non-inflatable lifejackets.

Recovering the MOB

This isn't always as easy as it sounds. Many years ago, for an afternoon 'round the cans' race, I shipped a crew whose principal asset was his girth. Deployed to windward in brisk weather his effects on stability were invaluable. I shall call him Albert.

Anyway, the race went well. We crossed the line at the head of the fleet and were returning to our berth in elated mood when Albert announced the need to relieve himself – adding that the facilities aboard my needle-hulled racing tri were so inadequately proportioned for a man of his stature that it would have to be al fresco.

He shambled aft towards the transom while we all looked the other way. Later he told us that he had grabbed what he thought to be the backstay to steady himself before leaning outboard to complete the task. It was then that he discovered two things: firstly that many trimarans don't have backstays in the traditional places and, secondly, that whip antennas are by nature … well … too whippy to be relied upon for support.

None of us saw it happen but a yelp followed by a very large splash signalled that Albert had unexpectedly left us. It soon became obvious that he was also a poor swimmer with a natural waterline somewhere just above his eyebrows. We got back to him soon enough and had him alongside but he was too heavy (and too furiously indignant) to get back on board. We eventually passed a sling under his arms, cleated him off to one of the floats, then motored into knee-deep water where he could regain the deck under his own steam. Sad to say, he lost his enthusiasm for sailing thereafter.

You will be relieved to learn there are more conventional methods you can employ.

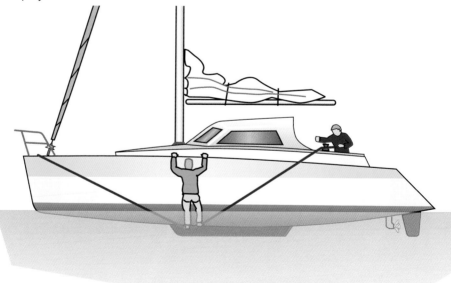

fig 9:2

RYA Multihull Handbook for cruisers

MOB recovery

Almost all modern catamarans have integrally moulded transom steps and these might seem to provide a readymade means of getting an MOB back on board. That could be the case in calm conditions but not if there's any type of sea running. It's true that multihulls barely roll at all but that doesn't mean they don't pitch. And, of course, when they do their sterns will rise and fall, well capable of delivering a hammer blow to anyone caught beneath. As if he hadn't had a bad enough day already.

Only choose this method if you believe there's little chance of injury. If in doubt, it's safer to take advantage of a catamaran's roll stability and recover the casualty from the side – preferably the leeward side – and about halfway along the boat. If the boat's freeboard is relatively modest and the casualty still physically capable, the simplest method is to rig a bight of rope from the bow to a sheet winch in the cockpit (fig 9:2). While someone cranks the winch, the MOB simply stands in the bight, taking any advantage of wave surge that might float him upwards and assisting as much as he can by gripping the gunwale and pulling himself upwards. Any spare crew should reach down and add their own muscle to drag him back onto the boat.

But this method is hard work for all concerned, not least the casualty. If he's in weakened condition, there's no alternative but to lift him directly upwards as shown in fig 9:3. Toss him the end of a halyard – the spinnaker halyard usually serves best – and ask him to tie a bowline under his arms. Better still, and far more comfortable for the casualty since they are invariably padded, is to use a dedicated sling (right). Crank on the winch and up he comes, again if possible helped over the guardwires by assisting crew.

If the dinghy is ready to hand – either afloat or very quickly deployable – it's sometimes easiest to use it as an intermediate step, heaving the MOB into it before transferring him to the greater security of the mother ship.

fig 9:3

9

Aftercare of the casualty

A person's normal body temperature is around 37°C (98.6°F). If it drops below 35°C (95°F) a casualty will be suffering hypothermia – an extremely dangerous and potentially fatal condition. The water temperature off England's south coast in early spring is about 8°C (46°F) so it's easy to see how someone could become hypothermic, though they may not be aware of it themselves.

Symptoms of hypothermia include:

■ Constant shivering

■ Lack of coordination

■ Slurred speech

■ General confusion

■ Drowsiness or apathy

■ Weak pulse and shallow breathing

■ Sinking into unconsciousness

Treated properly, the casualty should recover. Here's how:

■ Be extremely gentle with the person. Rough handling can induce cardiac arrest. Don't rub their limbs in an effort to warm them.

■ If possible, carefully move the casualty to a dry location out of the cold and wind.

■ Remove wet clothing. If necessary cut it off rather than risk unnecessary movement.

■ Lay the person on an insulated surface – a mattress or cockpit cushion is ideal – and cover with a blanket or similar. Leave only the face exposed.

■ Another person's body heat, applied skin to skin, is a good way to gently warm the casualty. They will forgive you the intimacy when they recover. It's their core body temperature you need to be concerned about. Warming the arms and legs can put additional stress on their heart.

■ If they are conscious and sufficiently alert, warm drinks will transfer heat to inside the body. The drink should be caffeine free and very definitely non-alcoholic. The traditional shot of brandy is a very bad idea.

■ Monitor the person's condition throughout. If they stop breathing you may need to administer cardiopulmonary resuscitation (CPR) of which, one hopes, every skipper will be familiar.

9

Fire extinguishers

There are few experiences more terrifying than fire at sea. Catamarans in particular tend to be distinctly compartmentalised and you may find yourself trapped. There should be an in-date fire extinguisher in every habitable compartment and a fire blanket in the galley. Engine spaces should have automatic extinguishers.

Remember, extinguishers in the conflagration area itself might become inaccessible, in which case you will be reliant on those you can actually lay your hands on.

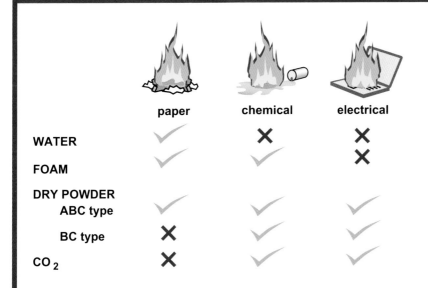

	paper	chemical	electrical
WATER	✓	✗	✗
FOAM	✓	✓	✗
DRY POWDER ABC type	✓	✓	✓
BC type	✗	✓	✓
CO$_2$	✗	✓	✓

Note: Halon extinguishers have been banned for environmental reasons but substitutes are available. Contact the manufacturers.

9

GLOSSARY

AFT: The rear end of a boat. The stern.

AKA: The beams that connect the three hulls of a trimaran.

AMA: The outer hulls of a trimaran. Also, the port hull of a double canoe.

ASPECT RATIO: The ratio between height and width – usually used to describe sails and foils such as daggerboards and rudders.

ATHWARTSHIPS: Lying or acting sideways across a boat.

BACK: To back a sail is to have it sheeted on the windward side so the sail's drive pushes a boat's bow around. Such a sail is said to be 'backwinded'.

BACKSTAY: Part of the standing rigging. A wire (or wires) that opposes the forces imposed by the 'forestay'.

BATTEN: A thin strip of a flexible material – usually plastic or glassfibre – to stiffen a sail and help support its 'roach'.

BEAM: A boat's width.

BEAM REACH: Sailing with the wind 'abeam' – i.e. coming directly from one side.

BEAR AWAY: To turn a sailboat away from the wind's direction.

BEAT: To sail as close to the wind's direction as possible. Also called 'close hauled'.

BOOM: A spar that supports and extends the bottom edge (the 'foot') of a sail – most commonly the mainsail.

BOW: The forward end of a hull.

BOWSPRIT: A pole extending forward of the bow, from which to attach a headsail's 'tack'.

BRIDGEDECK: The connecting platform that joins catamaran hulls.

BRIDLE: A pair of lines attached to an anchor warp or drogue line, intended to divide the load.

BROACH: To lose control and slew around so the boat lies side on to the waves.

BROAD REACH: A point of sail where the wind is from aft of the beam but not directly (or nearly) astern.

BULKHEAD: A structural lateral partition inside a hull.

CAPSIZE: Whoops!

CAR: A movable fairlead for a sheet, running athwartships for a mainsail and fore and aft for headsails.

CATAMARAN: A two hulled vessel.

CATENARY: The curve formed by a rope or chain suspended between points due to its weight. The shape taken up by an anchor rode is a good example.

CENTRE OF EFFORT: The geometric centre of a sail plan, used in stability calculations and other computations as a matter of convenience. The actual 'centre of aerodynamic force' depends largely on sail trim and is almost certainly elsewhere.

CENTRE OF LATERAL RESISTANCE: The geometric centre of a boat's immersed form, as seen from the side. This is another convenient approximation since, as above, the actual 'centre of hydrodynamic force' (the point at which a boat's resistance to leeway can be said to act) is again almost certainly elsewhere.

CENTREBOARD: A pivoting board that can be lowered into the water to help resist leeway.

CHAINPLATE: The attachment points on the hull for shrouds and stays.

CHINE: The angle formed between flat hull panels where they come together.

CLEAT: Used to secure lines. There are various different types.

CLEW: The bottom, aftmost corner of a sail.

CLOSE HAULED: See 'beat'.

CLOSE REACH: A point of sail somewhere between a beat and a beam reach.

COACHROOF: The raised part of the deck structure above the accommodation.

COCKPIT: The external control centre of a boat, both in terms of steering and sail trim.

CRUISING CHUTE: See 'spinnaker'.

CUTTER: A type of rig which carries a pair of headsails, one set behind the other.

DAGGERBOARD: A non-pivoting board that's lowered through a slot in a hull. Its purpose is to resist leeway.

DISPLACEMENT: The weight of water displaced by a boat afloat.

DOWNWIND: Sailing in the same general direction of the wind.

DROGUE: A drag device, towed astern to slow and help control a boat in heavy weather.

ESCAPE HATCH: A watertight hatch fitted into the side of a multihull's hull, that allows exit and entry after capsize.

FOLLOWING SEA: Waves coming from astern.

FOOT: The bottom edge of a sail.

FORESAIL: A sail set on the 'forestay' (see below). Usually smaller than a 'genoa' and often called a 'jib'.

FORESTAY: The foremost part of the standing rigging, leading from high on the mast to an attachment point on the centreline at deck level. It often carries a roller reefing gear.

FURL: To furl a sail is to roll it up. Please note that 'furling gears' are not necessarily 'reefing gears'.

GENOA: Any 'headsail' sail large enough to overlap the mast.

GOOSENECK: An articulated joint between the boom and mast.

GYBE: When sailing downwind, to alter course so that the sails must be set on the other side of the boat. Also spelled 'jibe'.

HALYARD: The rope used to raise and lower a sail.

HEAD: A sail's top corner.

HEADING: The direction you are sailing or would like to sail.

HEADSAILS: A general term describing any triangular sail set forward of the mast.

HEEL: The way a boat leans over, either from the wind or by a shift in weight. Keelboats do it abundantly; multihulls very little.

HELM: The steering mechanism. Also a politically correct term that avoids the distinction 'helmsman' or 'helmswoman'. Now you can say 'the helm is at the helm' should you feel the need. Don't expect much hilarity.

HOVE-TO: Lying nearly stationary in the water, usually with the foresail 'aback'. (See 'back'.)

JIB: A headsail that does not overlap the mast. Usually attached to the forestay.

JIBE: See 'gybe'.

KETCH: A two-masted sailboat with the shorter mast towards the stern.

KNOT: One nautical mile per hour. The oft-heard phrase 'knots per hour' is nonsensical since it would mean 'one nautical mile per hour per hour'.

LEE: The protected downwind side of an object.

LEE HELM: A balance between the hull shape and sailplan that will cause a boat to 'bear away' if the helm is released. Thoroughly undesirable.

LEE SHORE: Land that lies to 'leeward' of yourself. Not good news in heavy weather.

LEECH: The aft edge of a sail.

LEEWAY: The action of being pushed sideways as well as forward by the wind. Leeway represents lost progress when 'beating'.

LUFF: The foremost edge of a sail. 'To luff' means that edge starting to flutter when you sail too close to the wind.

NACELLE: A lowered area on the underside of a bridgedeck.

PARACHUTE ANCHOR: A sea anchor intended to minimise a boat's drift and hold it head to wind.

PITCHING: Fore and aft rocking motion.

PITCHPOLE: A form of capsize end-over-end or perhaps a little diagonally. Not reported to be much fun.

POINTING: Keeping the wing as close to the wind as possible. A boat that 'points high' will sail closer than one that 'points low'.

PORT: The left hand of a vessel when facing the bow.

POUNDING: The action of the seas 'pounding' on the underside of the hull or bridgedeck. Also known as 'slamming'. Not to be relished.

PREVENTER: A line rigged to hold the boom forward, thereby guarding against an accidental gybe.

PRODDER: See 'bowsprit'.

RAKE: The angle of the mast from the vertical.

REACH: See 'beam reach', 'broad reach' and 'close reach'.

REEF: To reduce sail area.

ROACH: The sail area that extends aftwards behind the straight line between the head and clew of a fore-and-aft sail. Usually refers to the mainsail.

RODE: A tether of some sort that connects a boat to an anchor, drogue or sea anchor. It can be of chain, rope or a combination of both. The last is a good compromise for multihulls.

ROLLER REEFING: A mechanism to reduce sail by winding it up around a small diameter spar – usually of aluminium.

RUNNING: Sailing downwind – i.e. with the wind coming from astern.

RUNNING RIGGING: Lines used to control sails, spars and mast bend. Usually rope but sometimes wire.

SHEETS: The primary control for the set of a sail – attached to the clew.

SHROUDS: The standing rigging – usually wire – that gives a mast athwartships support.

SLOOP: A single-masted sailboat which carries a single headsail.

SPINNAKER: A lightweight balloon type sail that's set 'flying' – that's to say not attached to a stay. Usually for downwind sailing but some types also capable of 'reaching'.

SPINNAKER POLE: A pivoting pole to which the 'tack' of a spinnaker is attached.

STARBOARD: The right hand side of a vessel when facing the bow.

STAY: Part of the standing rigging. A wire which supports the mast.

STAYSAIL: The aftmost headsail of a 'cutter' rig.

STERN: The rear of the boat.

SURF: The slide down a wave in the manner of a surfer.

TACK: The bottom front corner of a sail. Also, when going to windward, to alter course to put the wind on the other bow.

TELLTALE: A lightweight ribbon or other type of streamer that indicates the airflow over a sail.

TILLER: A handle or lever that operates the rudder for steering.

TOPPING LIFT: A line that takes the weight of a boom, preventing it from dropping.

TRAMPOLINE: A lightweight netting or fabric walkway between beams and/or hulls.

TRIMARAN: Sailboat with three hulls.

VANG: A tackle or other device between the mast and boom intended to hold the boom down. It controls mainsail leech tension. Also known as a 'kicking strap' or 'kicker'.

WEATHER (SIDE): The side onto which the wind blows.

WETTED SURFACE AREA: The area of the immersed porting of the hull.

WINDWARD: Towards the direction from which the wind blows.

WING MAST: A mast elongated in the fore-and-aft direction to form a rigid aerofoil. Such masts invariably rotate.

INDEX

RYA *Membership*

Promoting and Protecting Boating

www.rya.org.uk

RYA Membership

The RYA is the national organisation which represents the interests of everyone who goes boating for pleasure.

The greater the membership, the louder our voice when it comes to protecting members' interests.

Apply for membership today, and support the RYA, to help the RYA support you.

BENEFITS OF MEMBERSHIP

- Special members' discounts on a range of products and services including boat insurance, books, charts, DVD's and class certificates
- Access to expert advice on all aspects of boating from legal wrangles to training matters
- Free issue of Certificates of Competence, increasingly asked for by everyone from overseas governments to holiday companies, insurance underwriters to boat hirers
- Access to the wide range of RYA publications, including the quarterly magazine
- Third Party insurance for windsurfing members
- Free Internet access with RYA-Online
- Special discounts on AA membership
- Regular offers in RYA Magazine
- ...and much more

JOIN NOW

Membership form opposite or join online at www.rya.org.uk

Visit our website for information, advice, members' services and web shop.

IT'S ALL ABOUT YOU AND THE BOATING YOU DO

RYA MEMBERSHIP APPLICATION

Be part of it

One of boating's biggest attractions is its freedom from rules and regulations. As an RYA member you'll play an active part in keeping it that way, as well as benefiting from free expert advice and information, plus discounts on a wide range of boating products, charts and publications.

To join the RYA, please complete the application form below and send it to The Membership Department, RYA, RYA House, Ensign Way, Hamble, Southampton, Hampshire SO31 4YA. You can also join online at www.rya.org.uk, or by phoning the membership department on +44 (0) 23 8060 4159. Whichever way you choose to apply, you can save money by paying by Direct Debit. A Direct Debit instruction is on the back of this form.

	Title	Forename	Surname	Gender	Date of Birth
Applicant ❶					/ /
Applicant ❷					/ /
Applicant ❸					/ /
Applicant ❹					/ /

Address

Post Code

E-mail Applicant ❶

E-mail Applicant ❷

E-mail Applicant ❸

E-mail Applicant ❹

Home Tel   Day Time Tel   Mobile Tel

Type of membership required (Tick Box)

- Junior (0-11) Annual rate £5 or **£5 if paying by Direct Debit**
- Youth (12-17) Annual rate £14 or **£11 if paying by Direct Debit**
- Under 25 Annual rate £25 or **£22 if paying by Direct Debit**
- Personal Annual rate £43 or **£39 if paying by Direct Debit**
- Family* Annual rate £63 or **£59 if paying by Direct Debit**

Save money by completing the Direct Debit form overleaf

Please number up to three boating interests in order, with number one being your principal interest

- Yacht Racing
- Yacht Cruising
- Dinghy Racing
- Dinghy Cruising
- Personal Watercraft
- Sportboats & RIBs
- Windsurfing
- Motor Boating
- Powerboat Racing
- Canal Cruising
- River Cruising

Family Membership: 2 adults plus any under 18s all living at the same address. Prices valid until 30/9/2011. One discount voucher is accepted for individual memberships, and two discount vouchers are accepted for family membership.

IMPORTANT In order to provide you with membership benefits the details provided by you on this form and in the course of your membership will be maintained on a database. If you do not wish to receive information on member services and benefits please tick here ☐. By applying for membership of the RYA you agree to be bound by the RYA's standard terms and conditions (copies on request or at www.rya.org.uk)

Signature

Date   /   /

Source Code

Joining Point Code

PAY BY DIRECT DEBIT – AND SAVE MONEY

RYA

Be part of it

Instructions to your Bank or Building Society to pay by Direct Debit

Please fill in the form and send to:
Membership Department, Royal Yachting Association, RYA House, Ensign Way, Hamble,
Southampton, Hampshire SO31 4YA.

Name and full postal address of your Bank/Building Society

To the Manager

Address

Bank/Building Society

Postcode

Name(s) of Account Holder(s)

Branch Sort Code

– –

Bank/Building Society Account Number

Originator's Identification Number

9	5	5	2	1	3

RYA Membership Number (For office use only)

DIRECT Debit

Instructions to your Bank or Building Society

Please pay Royal Yachting Association Direct Debits from the account detailed in this instruction subject to the safeguards assured by The Direct Debit Guarantee. I understand that this instruction may remain with the Royal Yachting Association and, if so, details will be passed electronically to my Bank/Building Society.

Signature(s)

Date: / /